Be the Wisdom
YOU WANT TO SEE
IN YOUR KIDS

Be the Wisdom YOU WANT TO SEE IN YOUR KIDS

A Guide to Parenting with Inspiration,
Living with Joy, and Making a Difference

MAGDA TARNAWSKA SENEL, PH.D.

authorHOUSE®

AuthorHouse™
1663 Liberty Drive
Bloomington, IN 47403
www.authorhouse.com
Phone: 1 (800) 839-8640

Be the Wisdom You Want to See in Your Kids is not intended as a substitute for professional consultation in matters of childcare or parenting. It should be used only as a general guide and not as an ultimate source of information.

The author shall have neither liability nor responsibility to any person or entity with respect to any loss or damage caused, or alleged to have been caused, directly or indirectly, by the information contained in this book.

Published by AuthorHouse   10/01/2015

ISBN: 978-1-5049-0286-1 (sc)
ISBN: 978-1-5049-0285-4 (e)

Library of Congress Control Number: 2015904559

Print information available on the last page.

Illustrator Dan Drews
Cover by PixelStudio
Edited by David Tabatsky
Author's Photograph by Anna Uryga

This book is printed on acid-free paper.

PRAISE FOR *BE THE WISDOM YOU WANT TO SEE IN YOUR KIDS*

"Parents often know the theory for raising competent and happy children, but cannot apply it in challenging moments. Tarnawska's book closes this gap. Going beyond inspiration and theory Dr. Tarnawska Senel offers focused questions that are designed to bring on the parent's innate wisdom and emotional competence, as well as parent-child activities and poems to create connection and nurture the child's sense of self-worth. Following the book's instructions can bring peace, deep connection and joy into any relationship."

—Naomi Aldort, author of *Raising Our Children, Raising Ourselves.*

"In her meticulously crafted parenting guide, Dr. Tarnawska Senel not only weaves together mindful approaches to living and raising children, but thoughtfully shows us how to inspire our children to embrace these skills and perspectives with interactive exercises and poetry. Using a modern twist, Tarnawska shows us that the art of passing wisdom intergenerationally is alive and well."

—Bethany Casarjian, Ph.D., Clinical Director of Youth Services at the Lionheart Foundation, co-author of *Mommy Mantras* and *Power Source: Taking Charge of Your Life* and author of *Power Source Parenting: Growing Up Strong and Raising Healthy Kids.*

"Dr. Tarnawska Senel has written a refreshingly optimistic book that addresses the challenges of parenting in a manner that has the power to truly transform the experience of raising children. While she focuses on the uniqueness of each child, she also encourages parents to continually evolve in their own right in order to guide their children in their journey to self-discovery. A must read for every parent!"

—Nancy Lee Cecil, Ph.D., Professor of Education at California State University, Sacramento; expert on children's literacy and author of several books including *Striking a Balance: Comprehensive Approach to Literacy, Literacy in Grades 4-8,* and *Raising Peaceful Children in a Violent World.*

"Every page of this book has an idea, a real-life story, something to think about, a new concept to embrace, a new way to parent, and as the title promises, it indeed is a guide to parenting with inspiration, living with joy, and making a difference. I made lots of notes, scribbled in the margins, and turned down corners of pages I want to read again. You will be glad you stopped and took the time to read it. An insightful and very helpful book. I loved it!"

—Joyce Chapman, author of *Live Your Dream, Journaling For Joy* and *Celebrate Your Dream.*

"*Be the Wisdom You Want to See in Your Kids* is simultaneously deep and delightful, timeless and timely. As advocates and lifelong learners of conscious and soulful parenting, we love how Dr. Magda Tarnawska Senel, with refreshing humor and transparency, has so wisely woven a rich and relatable tapestry of parenting insights and hands-on activities for both parents and their children to enjoy – together. We highly recommend this as a daily workbook/playbook for grassroots mamas and papas who wish to learn and laugh, grow and s-t-r-e-t-c-h in mutuality with their kids, knowing that every day, every choice, every shared experience is sacred and pithy with the potential for deep learning and transformation."

—Einar C. Haver and Wennifer Lin Haver, Ph.D., co-creators of *The Water Brewery* http://www.thewaterbrewery.com and *Mother Tree Sanctuary* http://www.mothertreesanctuary.org

"*Be the Wisdom You Want to See In Your Kids* is a wonderful book using everyday issues parents face and turning them into simple, practical experiences children will learn and grow from. Dr. Tarnawska Senel eloquently leads parents on a deeper journey helping parents keep perspective and focus on what is really important. She masterfully and gently guides parents to look at parenting from a wellspring of their own values and wisdom to model to their children. A beautiful read!"

—Pilar Placone, Ph.D., Marriage and Family Therapist, author of *Mindful Parent Happy Child.*

For Timon

It's not our job to toughen our children up to face a cruel and heartless world. It's our job to raise children who will make the world a little less cruel and heartless.

— L.R. Knost

CONTENTS

*Parents need to fill a child's bucket of self-esteem so high
that the rest of the world can't poke enough holes to drain it dry.*

— Alvin Price

INTRODUCTION

It should come as no surprise that most people rate having children as the most meaningful and worthwhile experience of their lives. And yet, many parents often find themselves pushed to their limits, emotionally and physically. According to a recent Pew Research Center study, a majority of parents view childcare as a very exhausting activity. Many feel overwhelmed by the challenges of parenting on top of the multitude of everyday tasks and other obligations they already face.

Parents often struggle with feelings of guilt and inadequacy while trying to be perfect moms and dads, loving spouses or partners, competent employees, successful entrepreneurs, good friends, engaged citizens and fulfilled people. Most average human beings are unable to simultaneously meet all of these expectations. As a result, they end up living unfulfilling, cluttered and stressful lives. If this sounds familiar and you can relate to this in any way, this book is for you.

Be the Wisdom You Want to See in Your Kids is based on a simple premise—that happy and fulfilled parents raise happy and fulfilled children. It is meant to motivate parents to create inspired and joyful lives with their children while also serving as a supportive companion for those who may feel overwhelmed, depressed or simply in need of an energy boost. The book's main value lies in its optimism and wisdom and with the creative activities it provides for parents and children. It encourages parents to discover their most authentic and inspired self through the actual experience of parenting. This may lead to satisfying the universal desire that all parents have to raise joyful, happy and successful children who can develop to their fullest potential.

When we become parents, everything changes. It is not only that new, extra person in the house to suddenly figure out and take care of; it really becomes about how we deal with becoming different people ourselves, as we grow and stretch and come to view relationships and the world around us through an extraordinarily expanded lens.

Parenthood affords us the opportunity to become more compassionate, patient and understanding, but we also run the risk of becoming irritable, impatient and intolerant. Yikes! We had better become aware of those risks and *do* something to approach these changes in conscious and responsible ways. So this is not merely a parenting book with instructions on how to raise your child. It's more about raising you, hopefully to a more holistic, healing place of empowerment and inspiration.

Several years ago, through my own experience as a new mother and in conversations with other parents, I realized there was a great need for a parenting book that embraced the notion that a parent must continue to evolve in his or her own right while simultaneously cultivating a deep relationship with his or her child.

Specific issues repeatedly surfaced, including the need to reboot one's life and identity after becoming a parent, the difficulties in dealing with new challenges, and a desire to develop a more holistic and mutually satisfying relationship with one's child. I came to realize that aspiring to raise a joyful and thriving child while also seeking to elevate oneself to a place of empowerment and inspiration should not be mutually exclusive.

Most researchers agree that the foundation for happiness and success in life is set in childhood and that some of the most important contributing factors are a positive self-image, confidence in one's abilities, an optimistic outlook, healthy self-discipline and good relationships with people. Naturally, I want all of these things for my son, Timon (rhymes with Simon), who is now six years old and, thankfully, sleeping as I write.

So I keep asking myself, what is the difference between a person who is unable to live a happy and fulfilling life and one who succeeds in living with enthusiasm, grace and a rich feeling of fulfillment? How do we arrive at adulthood behaving the way we do? This question really pops up at high school reunions. When I went to my 20th recently (ouch!), I was struck by how the current lives of my classmates and friends were an obvious reflection of the personalities, attitudes and beliefs they displayed during our high-school years. Looking back, the development of their personal and professional lives seems quite predictable. I also found confirmation that a positive self-image, confidence in one's abilities, an optimistic outlook on life, healthy self-discipline, and good relationships with people are absolutely crucial and that, in addition to natural personality-based inclinations, these qualities are either acquired and nurtured in their families or never learned at all.

This book explores these themes through a series of reflections on how we perceive and experience our daily lives. It also includes poetry and illustrations intended as conversation starters for adults and children. (Don't worry if you disliked poetry back in school or simply didn't understand it. You will not have any trouble with the poems in this book. I promise!)

What is more important than instilling ideas of self-love and self-worth in our children? Those are two pillars of raising happy and healthy children, but we must also promote healthy habits, excitement for learning and a positive outlook on life. We can do this by nurturing respect for other people and for nature; conveying the importance of gratitude; looking at life through the prism of opportunities (rather than failures); and always doing our individual best. Once we—and our children—begin practicing these habits, we can further appreciate the importance of family, embrace diversity and explore more spiritual connections in our life.

The simple principles in this book reinforce concepts of mindful and soulful parenting, meant to strengthen the mind, body and spirit of both children and parents. But what I hope makes this book truly useful is in providing ways to actively build these foundations *with* your children.

Be the Wisdom You Want to See in Your Kids presents several proven models for effectively achieving higher levels of fulfillment, including the practice of mindfulness, guided visualization, journaling, creating and using mantras, using humor to discharge negative situations and living in the mode of *being* and *allowing* versus *doing* and *forcing*.

Each chapter begins with a narrative for parents that explores an emotion or attitude that is at the core of the human experience, with titles such as Developing Confidence, Nurturing Talents, Cultivating Gratitude, Learning to Yield, Respecting Life, Celebrating Differences, Letting Go of Fear and Accepting Change, and offers guidance in developing empowering attitudes and concepts.

This is followed by two sections called "Diving Deeper," a series of questions meant to challenge and inspire you to delve further into the process of self-discovery and "Getting Active," with some suggested activities for you that might help transform everyday tasks into more fulfilling and mindful activities. Since this book is meant to be convenient and easy to use, there is space allotted for writing your answers and thoughts.

Once you've had some precious and necessary "me time," it's time to bring your family together in a section called "Conversation Starters to Engage Your Child." First, you will find an illustration and a poem that reinforce the chapter's theme, followed by "Getting Active Together," consisting of a variety of suggested activities to perform with your child. Children respond differently to a variety of stimuli. Some prefer visual content while others enjoy poetry, word games or storytelling. In the end, what's most important is that you and your child can share art, words and activities together.

Each chapter is intentionally short. After all, when you are the parent of a young child, who has the time, energy or even an interest in reading a tome or textbook? With this book, however, you can read an entire chapter before, during or after engaging your child with the usual bedtime fare, or take the book along on a picnic or bus ride, where short-and-sweet are best.

It can be very empowering and uplifting to insert a bit of wisdom and reflection into our busy lives, especially if they help to create a more mindful approach to living. I am a strong believer in the creative power each of us possess to manifest all desires—given the right spiritual and psychological foundation, attitude and self-discipline.

Initially, I wrote this book for my son and for myself. While reading stories to my son, I have often wished there would be something in those books for me, too, something relevant written especially for me, and, even better, suggestions for how I could share its meaning with my son through purposeful activities. And vice versa—while reading words of wisdom in fiction, philosophy or parenting books, I wondered how I could translate these bits of insight into something my son would understand. As a result, I have created the book I wished already existed, one I can ponder for myself and share with my child.

When Timon was born, I discovered—maybe for the first time in my life—how profound and unconditional love can be, touching the deepest level of my soul, felt in every cell of my body and vibrating behind every thought I had. I felt it when I was holding him close to my heart and when he was sleeping peacefully in his bed. That love was there when I was thinking about him, feeding him, changing his diaper and when he kept me up at night. And it remained inside me everywhere I went, more important than anything else I had ever known.

But while raising Timon through everyday routines and experiences, I also had to fight irritation, annoyance and unwelcome habitual reactions. I was forced to transform my fears into empowering forces, which meant summoning up all of my determination, patience and flexibility. In other words, I had to conquer myself. I also learned that ordinary, day-to-day life with its commonplace routines can be the source of our greatest challenges, including stagnation, depression and destructive thoughts; but if approached mindfully and soulfully, these challenges can also produce magic, fulfillment and joy.

I am still learning to *choose* empowering attitudes, healthy habits and the courage and desire to shine bright like the sun amidst the ups and downs of everyday life. I am also doing my best to model these choices for my son. But it is not always easy and I fail at times. Then, I remind myself that soulful parenting, leading a fulfilling life and creating a more peaceful world do not just happen by themselves; they are a result of choices we make every day, with each one hopefully bringing us closer to the life that we desire.

My deepest wish is that this book may help other parents and children co-create mutual, wonderfully fulfilling relationships, setting the foundation for a magnificent life.

I like to tell Timon that the best thing he can do is to be himself and not to try to be like somebody else. I hope each of you will find your connection to this philosophy and to others in this book, and that you enjoy sharing them with a child you love.

Each of us is a unique strand in the intricate web of life and here to make a contribution.

— Deepak Chopra

1

Being Me

"Your son is six and he can't swim?"

I nodded to my friend, Jennifer, already dreading what this could mean.

"Really, Magda," she continued. "I just saw a three-year old diving in the pool like a fish."

I groaned.

"You have to teach Timon how to swim before it's too late."

"Too late for what"—I thought—"for making the Olympic swimming team in ten years?"

I could laugh at that notion but not at my son's inability to swim, because what if it meant I was failing to live up to the idea of being a perfect parent?

On other occasions, my friend pointed out that Timon's handwriting was still a bit wobbly or that he couldn't stay seated in a restaurant without running around the table every two minutes.

I cringed with self-doubt. Maybe Timon needed a better swimming teacher or a daily writing tutor. Maybe I should have already taken him to see a child psychologist to find out why he cannot sit quietly for extended periods of time.

"You know, my neighbor dropped by yesterday with her two grandkids," Jennifer continued, "and they were so well-behaved and pleasant to be around."

As I looked at Timon jumping around and laughing, I suddenly came to my senses. His personality and development are as unique as his fingerprint and he cannot—and should not—be measured according to anyone else's notion of what is "normal" or "appropriate."

Equally important, I also decided to give myself the option of being *me*—the parent I am. Each of us, Timon and me—and any child and parent for that matter—are unique in nature, determined not only by each of our extraordinary experiences, but through our everyday living and learning situations: enjoyable, mundane, and tedious, too. Managing our lives—despite emotional overload, habitual reactions and the need for instant gratification—is a skill. Molding our individuality—by choosing to consistently create the best version of ourselves through a life of soulful reflection—is an art.

This is not to say that we should not teach our children how to swim, write or behave in a restaurant. Rather, it is about looking at our children through the prism of their individuality and finding what is most suitable for them—taking into account the well-meaning advice of our relatives, friends and experts, but more importantly, listening to our own hearts. When we consider the singular abilities, temperaments, talents, and gifts of our children and ourselves, we simply cannot apply the same measuring stick to everyone.

From the moment our babies first discovers that they have fingers and toes, they enter a path of self-discovery one can hope will last throughout their entire life. As parents, we must commit ourselves to supporting our children's sense of uniqueness and special purpose in life, and we can begin this with them at an early age, when they are already developing faster than we can almost comprehend. This is the time to teach them how to cherish their unique qualities, and as they do, they will eventually come to appreciate the value and purpose of their life, leading to a desire to live in joy and make meaningful contributions to the world.

This is the essence of a fulfilling, inspired and happy life, one that adds value to the world, and expands the fullness of our beings while allowing us to enjoy the journey. This can occur when one's unique nature fits well with one's direction in life.

The maxim "Know thyself," inscribed at the legendary temple of Apollo in Delphi, Greece roughly 2500 years ago, was created for good reason. Acknowledging ourselves as part of our world and claiming our distinctive role in life is not possible without discovering and consciously creating who we truly are. As parents, it is our responsibility—and great pleasure—to expose our children to this idea so that it becomes a brightly shining core in every child. It must begin with each of us, as role models to our children. The better we know ourselves, the more aware we are of our own uniqueness and purpose, and the more committed we can be to being true to ourselves. When this occurs—in real time—our core becomes more radiant and shines that much brighter.

Internal peace and harmony are not meant to be the exclusive domain of the Buddhas. Each of us has the potential to choose this path and expand our lives to experience it on a daily basis. As we learn to do this, we increase our passion for life and deepen our relationships to other people and the environment in which we live. That awareness and celebration of life will lead us to a genuine interest in making this world a better place—in small, medium and very large ways.

When our children mirror our behavior, they begin defining their own vision of what makes life meaningful. Hopefully, each of them will summon up the courage to follow their dreams and manifest their desires in seemingly miraculous ways.

This process does not happen by itself. When we see people living in harmony with themselves and the world around them, it appears so natural and effortless—and perhaps it is, at least in the moments we are witnessing. They seem to exist with such lightness and ease, but I am convinced that their peace of mind and tranquility is the result of a dedicated series of intentions, maybe even shaped during childhood, that focus on creating high self-esteem, a positive self-image and confidence in one's abilities.

Children that are introduced to these concepts at a young age are very fortunate. They have been nurtured and encouraged—most likely by their parents—to believe in their abilities and the endless possibilities life presents. Raising children this way allows them to explore their passions, leading them to discover who they really are and to cherish their unique qualities.

No matter how tough life may seem sometimes, we parents must not dim our own light. We all have a divine spark inside—be it our soul or higher self—inviting the good and heroic parts of us to come forth and deliver. When we are able to recognize the divine source of our uniqueness, trust the intuitive guidance and align with our life purpose then we can claim our personal power, live in the fullness of our being, radiate our magnificence and make a difference in the world.

In other words, we ought to feel compelled to live joyfully, enthusiastically, purposefully and meaningfully, and by doing so we become capable of inspiring others—like our children—to aspire to be their best possible selves and live their best possible lives.

This concept appears simple enough but it is very difficult to actualize within our demanding, almost bipolar culture. From an early age, we are encouraged to compete on the one hand and conform on the other. But how is this possible? For better or for worse, as if we just can't help ourselves, we want to have bigger cars, nicer bodies, smarter kids and better jobs than our neighbors. At the same time, we are often subconsciously afraid that if we stand out and are more successful than our peers, family or friends, we will either be taken advantage of or rejected.

To live mindfully is not about competing, pitting ourselves against others to prove who is "better" at math or science—or parenting. What does "better" even mean, let alone "success"? To live mindfully is to discover what is really important to us, nurture it on a daily basis and make choices that align with these values.

So should I be concerned if my child does not make the Olympic team? Naturally, the world is a competitive place and a certain amount of rivalry is necessary to gain the glory manifested in awards, titles and compensation. But what is any of that worth if it merely supports an ego trip at the expense of self-actualization, ever-expanding joy and a sense of genuine fulfillment?

While the competition model often generates a lot of unnecessary envy, bitterness and resentment directed toward the front-runner; the self-development model is more inclusive, as it inspires, motivates, and empowers anyone open to its value. If we celebrate our differences—not to prove we are better than anyone else but simply to express our inborn uniqueness and fulfill our life purpose—then we can experience a joy and fulfillment that will overflow into other people's lives and uplift them.

Our goal should be about becoming the best possible version of ourselves in alignment with our core values—without the need for comparing ourselves with others. This is a philosophy worth introducing to our children from a very early age.

Diving Deeper

Philosophy is nice––it helps us reflect and understand the world around us––but planting a seed for a flower to grow may be better. It has tangible results! As parents, we must cultivate good ideas about raising our children, but what we *do* is what really counts. In this spirit, here are a few questions––and space to write your thoughts:

1. If we assume that none of us is on our planet by accident but has some kind of mission to fulfill, what is yours? (Is it to add more beauty, kindness or joy to the world, to raise your child to find the fullness of his or her being, to contribute to a tangible form of positive transformation?) What is your mission? What would you like that mission to be?

2. Are you aware of your own importance in the world and your potential to make a difference in other people's lives? An encouraging word or a willing ear might mean the world to someone.

3. How do you celebrate your own "magnificent individuality"? (If the notion of magnificent individuality feels like a stretch, identify why and ask yourself how you would celebrate it, if you believed in your own magnificence.)

4. Do you aspire to be your best possible self, not compete with others to prove anything, but to express your inborn uniqueness? How can you teach your child to do the same?

Getting Active

The answers to these questions reside within us. Clarity often arrives when we remove any inner obstacles blocking our awareness. As we try creating our individual responses to these questions, some of these strategies might be helpful.

1. What makes you *you*? Give yourself at least 15 minutes of uninterrupted time to make a list, a luxury for some, no doubt, but a necessary gift you deserve.

A. Five things you like about yourself:

B. Five values most important to you:

C. Five things you want to experience:

D. Five actions you would like to take to make a difference in the world:

2. Some of us become limited by feeling that we are not good, organized, smart, successful, educated, attractive, important, lovable, disciplined or competent *enough*. Which of these limiting beliefs do you perceive as "truth" about yourself? One way to

identify them is to think of all the reasons (read: excuses) you come up with for not following your dreams.

3. How would lifting these limits change your life? What would you do and who would you be without these beliefs?

4. What can you actively do to declare your first step toward being magnificent?

Conversation Starters to Engage Your Child

Being Me

Do you know who I am? Do you see what I see?
I am very special! There's no one like me.
So call me unique, please, and wonderful, too.
Just cherish me daily; that's all you must do.

With my family's support, I enjoy being me.
They give blessings and praise, so I'm happy and free,
With my generous heart and my fanciful mind,
You can say that I'm truly one of a kind!

So whenever I struggle to make a good choice,
I listen real hard to my own special voice.
What should I do now, or what shall I say?
That's true to myself, and that's really my way?

Each day of my life gives me joy and a smile.
No question about it: I'm one lucky child.
Do you know who I am? Do you see what I see?
I'm the singular, wonderful, marvelous me!

Getting Active Together

1. Start a conversation with your child by asking: "How many girls or boys do you know who have the same name as you? How many of them have the same hair color and style? How many look exactly like you? How many have the same toys? How many of them live where we live?" Reiterate how special and unique every person is, beginning, of course, with your own child. Recognizing—and role modeling—your own magnificent individuality will help your child do the same.

2. Try an art project I have enjoyed with my son. Cut your child's body shape out of cardboard and fill it up with drawings, words and magazine cutouts representing his or her special qualities and interests. For example, Timon drew stick figures representing his family and best friends and a big red heart as a symbol of his love for them. He glued pictures from magazines representing things he enjoys doing and learning about as well as all of the nice things he does at home or school and the special places we have visited.

3. Together with your child, make a list of things he or she likes and enjoys doing, topics of interest, favorite songs, and other activities

you both think would be fun to try out. Stretch yourself a bit and put things on the list that you have never done before together. Experience the excitement of doing something new at least once a month. Following this path I was able to explore many remarkable things and places with my family, such as participating in a Lavender Festival, a children's book festival, visiting a garden dedicated to peace and all world religions, museum exhibits and animal rescue centers.

Self-confidence is the first requisite to great undertakings.

— Samuel Johnson

2

Developing Confidence

During a family trip to Hawaii, we decided to hike to the top of Diamond Head. In spite of the hot weather and lack of shade on the trail, it was quite a pleasant day––but not for Timon. Barely ten minutes into our walk, he started complaining that he was tired and did not want to continue. My husband and I were not eager to carry him all the way to the top. Determined to finish what we started, I tried to remember one of the numerous tips I had gathered from friends and parenting books that would help me through this challenge. When that failed, I tried tapping into my own creativity to come up with a solution. It was becoming hotter and our pace was certainly slowing when an idea struck. Could we hike more easily to the top if I engage Timon in a mental activity that is meaningful and appealing to him?

First, in an effort to empower my son, I nominated him as our leader, in charge of leading us to the top of Diamond Head. As our pace naturally picked up, we started looking at rocks and guessing what shapes they were, and counted our steps and talked about the relative strength of different animals. These simple activities––along with his newfound sense of responsibility––enabled Timon to enjoy the hike––so much so that he soon began walking almost without a break, hopping around the trail without even feeling the increasing heat. All the while, he was sharpening his analytical thinking skills by figuring out, for example, how many giraffes could pull one dinosaur on a sled and how many horses would be needed to transport ten elephants up the mountain. When we arrived at the top without any more interruptions or complaints, we were able to admire spectacular views of Oahu's coastline. Feeling more refreshed than I could have ever even hoped for, we walked back down in a joyful mood.

Observing Timon's excitement, I remembered my grandfather, who, while taking me on long mountain hikes when I was child, infused me with a love of adventure. He inspired me to learn about nature by exploring and respecting it. He also gave me a lot of confidence in my physical capabilities, by always gently pushing me to walk further than I thought I could, to go forward even if I felt somewhat scared and to believe in things most people thought were unattainable. I was fortunate to learn at a young age that I could push myself beyond what I perceived as my limits and question whether things that seemed impossible were really out of my reach.

On the day we hiked up Diamond Head, three lessons emerged, which have become valuable tools applicable to both my parenting and personal growth. The first lesson pertains to our human ability to alter the perspective through which we look at any potentially boring, strenuous or unpleasant activity that may become advantageous in the long run or cannot be avoided. The second lesson reveals the importance of guiding our children to discover their own endurance and confidence in their abilities. The third lesson comes from my grandfather, who was able to enter the world of a child's imagination in a way that does not occur to most adults. This created a very special bond between us during my childhood and shaped me in many positive ways, which I try to emulate in my relationship with Timon.

When we engage children in activities they don't necessarily enjoy in a way that makes these undertakings exciting for them, we can teach them about the power of the mind to change their viewpoint. And it all starts with us as parents and how we demonstrate our ability and self-discipline in reframing unpleasant but necessary everyday tasks and obligations.

During a seminar I attended once on spirituality, leadership and money, the teacher T. Harv Eker shared a personal story about the power of changing the way we look at things. One of the household tasks he absolutely abhorred was taking out the trash, but when he and his wife divided the housework it became his chore. In order to survive the ordeal, he decided that every time he had to take out the trash he would think of it as a gift for his wife, and of how happy she would be that she did not have to do it herself. Instead of focusing on the stinky trash, he saw the happy and smiling face of his wife, which ultimately made a tremendous difference in how he felt about his chore.

I have applied this principle many times and it works splendidly, especially when I have been creative and energetic enough to come up with a suitable scenario. So when Timon needed to practice writing his alphabet letters, which he resisted fiercely at first, instead of forcing him to do it, I enticed him to pretend that he was fulfilling a task of writing a secret message that would lead us to discover a pirate's treasure. He ended up enjoying the task so much that he stayed involved in the activity for more than forty minutes without demanding a break.

So why should reaching the peak only be the goal of mountain climbers?

Challenges we face on a daily basis can teach our children the importance of focusing on our ultimate goal, believing in ourselves and not giving up. How we as parents respond to challenges will often determine what our children learn about motivation, persistence and determination.

I have often cited our Diamond Head hike to demonstrate to Timon that even when the road becomes difficult we can still keep going forward until we reach the peak. We may complain a little or desperately count each step, but giving up is not an option. This lesson becomes more universal when applied to other situations, such as difficulties in school or an initial inability to master a new skill.

Setting worthwhile goals and persisting until we accomplish them will usually increase self-confidence and our belief in the ability to learn and succeed will become stronger each time. Creating safe situations where we can experience something out of the ordinary with our children, such as those I experienced with my grandfather, will help us feel more connected, playful and vibrant.

Some of the more intricate adventures my grandfather shared with me when I was six or seven involved walking through wetlands and tall corn dog grass that surrounded a remote lake. We did this so that we could sneak into a fisherman's boat and free the worms imprisoned in a rusty can. We also fed a flock of sheep in a wild pasture and searched for a magical fern flower in the woods that, according to an eastern European legend, had the power to fulfill every wish of the person who was courageous and lucky enough to find it.

Every time I embark on an adventure with Timon and put aside the serious demeanor of a grown-up, I see happy sparkles in his eyes. In those moments, I feel more alive and radiant, too. Our sense of adventure has led us to following a trash truck through the streets of Los Angeles and applauding the sanitation workers at each of their stops, hiking to a hidden waterfall and exploring the Crystal Cave in Sequoia National Forest.

Each of these experiences included a set of challenges, either for me ("I hope I won't meet any of my colleagues while applauding sanitation workers performing their job") or for my son ("What if a there is a monster in the cave?") that we were able to conquer. One important aspect of believing in one's abilities is being aware of the creative power of words and how important it is to be mindful of what we say. When it comes to our abilities and possibilities, we often become what we keep telling ourselves.

When Timon says, "I will never be able to do this," or "I never get what I want," I remind him that his words are very powerful. So I was stunned when one day out of the blue he responded to me complaining that I don't have enough time by saying, "Mama, remember, words are very powerful."

We have the power to achieve great success in any area of our life and it all starts with thoughts and words, followed by action and determination. As I am conveying this concept to Timon, I learn and re-learn along with him by becoming more mindful of my own thoughts, words, choices and actions.

Diving Deeper

These questions can help us examine how we approach demanding situations and reflect on ways we can grow as human beings, by exercising the power of our minds to look at things in a more empowering light. Once we begin doing that, we can guide our children to do the same.

1. By observing how you respond to challenges, what will your child learn about motivation, persistence and determination?

2. How can you help your child build more confidence in his or her abilities? How can you motivate and inspire more learning?

3. How can you teach your child about the power of the mind to change our perspective on every situation?

Getting Active

While there is no cookie cutter approach for responding to these questions, we can find more meaningful answers if we utilize these simple techniques.

1. Be aware of how you respond to obstacles. Recall a challenge you recently faced and write down the thoughts you had when you encountered that challenge for the first time, all the steps you took (or did not take) to overcome it, and the final result. What did you learn from the situation? How can you apply this lesson in the future?

2. Make a list of things you consider to be your greatest achievements. Keep adding to your list as you remember more. Start a journal where you write five accomplishments each day and congratulate yourself for each one of them. This exercise was shared with me by Teresa Romain from accessabundance.com and worked miracles in my own sense of accomplishment.

3. Make a list of fun, creative and engaging things you have done that made you feel joyful, vibrant and happy. They don't have to

be elaborate adventures like climbing Kilimanjaro or going white water rafting on the Magpie River. They should be things that were truly exciting for *you*, something as simple as taking a walk on a warm rainy day. Try to add one thing to your list each month.

Conversation Starters to Engage Your Child

Developing Confidence

If you're looking at me and you think I am small,
You'd better look twice, 'cause I really am tall.
It's only a question of confidence, see;
You're as big as you feel, so just feel big like me!

There are so many things I can do all alone,
Without any help, in my confident zone,
Like making a sculpture and stacking those blocks
And dressing myself from my head to my socks.

I'm learning each day about spiders and bees
And what squirrels like to do at the top of the trees.
When teachers start teaching, it's my lucky day;
I learn how to work and find good ways to play.

At home with my parents, I chance things and try.
I shrug and just wing it; I don't know quite why.
Maybe I'm learning to choose my own way
That helps me feel stronger, I really must say.

Getting Active Together

1. Design an adventure involving an appropriate challenge to experience with your child. Planning the adventure together is a great first step. Anticipate some of the difficulties and ask your child how he or she could overcome them. During the adventure, encourage your child to reach just a little beyond his or her perceived limits. Take pictures of different parts of the road. Make an album, documenting the difficulties and the achievements as you both finally reach your combined goal.

2. Revisit an activity that your child did not like the first time. Help him or her redefine the activity or change the focus, leading to a fresh look and a new approach.

3. Go to a bookstore or library with your child and look through magazines or books in the travel section. Find a place you both would be really excited to visit and start finding out more about that place. Make a board or a journal with all of the ideas and pictures. Keep adding to it any time you feel like.

Anyone who has never made a mistake
has never tried anything new.

— Albert Einstein

3

Doing My Best

I once read a story about a successful scientist who attributed his choice of career and the desire to experiment to the influence and parenting skills of his mother. To demonstrate her way of relating to him, he tells a story about how as a child he once spilled milk on the kitchen floor. Instead of reprimanding him or demanding that he clean it up immediately, his mother concluded that since the milk had been already spilled, they might as well have some fun and find a way to play with it before cleaning up. It must have been a lot of milk because, if I remember his story correctly, they floated paper boats on the milk and moved them around the floor.

What I found extraordinary was the willingness of his mother to let go of any urge to clean up the kitchen immediately or to reprimand her child, both of which for many of us would have probably been a habitual reaction. Instead, she chose to engage her son in what they could do together to turn this ordinary and somewhat negative experience into something positive and exciting. This story has stuck with me for a long time because the mother's response was not something I ever observed as a child or saw myself having as a parent.

It's quite remarkable what a child can learn from this reaction, namely, that there is nothing wrong with failing while trying to do something worthwhile, that there is always a lighthearted and playful way to deal with mistakes, that a potentially unpleasant situation can be turned into a positive happening and that missteps can lead to new discoveries. As a matter of fact, many inventions were made as a result of an error, mix-up or a misstep—amazing creations, such as penicillin, x-rays, microwaves, fireworks and ink-jet printers, to name a few.

Mistakes are just that: mis-takes that may—or may not—lead to new discoveries or original ways of looking at things. But even if they do not contribute to any earth-shattering inventions or insights, they will always be an integral part of our human experience.

Accepting this and learning from our missteps—and not beating ourselves up for them— is the best we can do. Conveying this message to our children and helping them internalize it is worth trying, as is reflecting on our own slipup. Considering our upbringing, circumstances, emotional state and level of awareness (to list just a few variables), don't we (almost) always aim to do the best we can— in every situation?

Although we all know that it is not possible to make a game of it every time our child spills, breaks or drops something, it is important to find ways to lighten up and turn at least some of these situations into something fun, positive and empowering.

Using humor to discharge the negativity from a situation is still not something that comes easily to me. I need to remember to be mindful and consciously choose my reactions, which of course is not always possible. But when I *do* remember to use humor, miracles happen.

Timon recently refused to put on his shoes when we were about to leave for school. Oblivious to the fact that we were running late and unconcerned about several appointments I had already lined up, he decided that he did not like his shoes anymore and would prefer to stay at home. Holding my to-do list for the day that included more tasks than could be accomplished in one week, I wasn't in a very relaxed or easy-going state of mind.

"We really have to go, sunshine," I said, trying to hide my impatience with a calm veneer of composure. "We will be late if we don't hurry."

"No. I don't want to."

My irritation suddenly rose to a new height when Timon ran to hide in his room.

"Don't you understand that I have so much to do and need to run to a doctor's appointment after dropping you off at school?"

I knew that his innocent lack of concern would not allow him to understand the importance of my to-do-list. Just as I was about to scream in desperation, I realized that we both were trying to accomplish what each of us saw as a priority. Was my agenda more important? Of course it was. Wasn't it? At the end of the day, I was the one responsible for managing our daily lives and making sure that everyone's needs and obligations in the family were being met—on top of all of the other commitments, projects and aspirations I had. So wasn't my agenda more important?

"Why doesn't he get it?" I thought angrily.

Then I remembered that any agitation and stress I was feeling would not help. In fact, it would only exacerbate my anxiety and Timon's resistance. So I tried a different angle.

"Okay Timon," I said loud enough for him to hear me in his room. "You can wear my shoes and I will put on yours."

I took his shoe and started putting it on my foot with a serious face. I made a show of huffing and puffing and talking to the shoe, trying very hard to squeeze my foot in. Surprised by my sudden change of heart, Timon came back and was observing my efforts with a puzzled look on his face. In a moment, he started smiling. I watched his brain at work.

"Mama, this shoe is too small for you. You better put on your own shoes and I will put on mines."

I was already running late for my appointments and did not get to number five on my to-do list that day, but I was able to lighten up a bit and avoided generating a lot of additional negativity that would have affected me and my son on many different levels. Maybe I even saved other people that day from becoming easy targets for my emotional outbursts or sarcastic remarks—like that guy who cut me off on the freeway and then mysteriously appeared in the post office parking lot to take the spot I was coveting, or the cashier at Home Depot who felt that flirting with her co-worker was more important than helping me through the self-checkout.

Either way, I had to wonder how I was managing myself on this rollercoaster of emotions. Was I doing something I should feel bad about? Or even worse, should I be feeling bad about myself?

In her research and work on parenting, Dr. Brené Brown introduces the important distinction between guilt and shame. Guilt is an awareness that one has done something wrong or inappropriate and a feeling of regret for acting in this particular way. Shame is a belief that there is something fundamentally wrong with the person for acting in a certain way. It is very important to teach children to make this distinction and infuse them with the idea that they are always worthy of love and acceptance no matter how many mistakes they make. Brown cautions parents not to use shame as a parenting tool and talks about a study conducted on young children to see if they also used shame or guilt-based language. The study followed the children throughout the college years and found out that children who were using shame-based language were much more prone to drop out of college or succumb to addictions.

So why might it be good to spill a little milk every once in a while?

How we react to the mistakes or misbehaviors of our children can have long-lasting consequences, either helping them to choose more productive behaviors in the future by confirming their self-worth or increasing the chance of them acting out as a result of the instilled feeling of inferiority. It can also make or break our own day!

Diving Deeper

Making the distinction between guilt and shame, using humor to discharge potentially adverse situations and not beating ourselves up for things we could have done differently are valuable principles that apply to parents and children. Answering the following questions can lead to gaining clarity about where we fall short and help us practice better habits on a daily basis.

1. How can you remember to choose to be more open-minded and lighthearted in challenging situations?

2. How do you stay mindful of your thoughts, emotions, words and behavior when irritation and agitation arise?

3. Do you use shame or guilt-based language when talking to yourself and to your child?

4. How can you turn mistakes or mishaps into teaching moments for self-worthiness, creativity and humor?

Getting Active

Thinking of some approaches ahead of time to discharge stressful and escalating situations can be helpful in accomplishing that task.

1. The next time your child breaks, spills or drops something unintentionally, see if you can find humor in the situation or use it creatively to add more playfulness to your life. Start by counting to ten in your mind before doing or saying anything you may wish later that you could take back.

2. Whenever you catch yourself or your child using shame-based language ("I can't believe I locked myself out of the house. How could I be so stupid?"), reiterate the statement to make a

distinction between the action and yourself ("I am smart, even though forgetting to take the key was not.")

3. When another person is getting upset and you become the target of his or her emotional outburst or impoliteness, set the limit, but don't take it personally. It's usually not about you. It is about the other person's stress, dissatisfaction with life or a million other undesirable things that could be going in their lives. Sometimes, a genuine "I am sorry you are having a bad day" can work wonders.

Conversation Starters to Engage Your Child

Doing My Best

When I spill milk or drop stuff or simply fall down,
I might cry or get bothered or maybe just frown.
But this is okay, I really must say;
I change what looks bad to a reason to play.

So listen real good, 'cause here's how it's done:
I'm sharing my secrets, starting with one.
When I fall on the floor, I always get up.
I clean up my mess, like the milk or a cup.

And once that's all finished, it's time to play more,
With pans, pots and fire trucks all over the floor.
We all make mistakes; that's what we all do,
But it's really no reason to stand up and boo.

So whenever I stumble or drop stuff, I say,
Just shrug and clean up and get on with your day.
So that's what I do when I'm put to test.
I always do great when I'm doing my best!

Getting Active Together

1. A strategy that works wonders is an agreement I made with my son: Any time one of us feels like screaming, instead of following through on this impulse, we give each other a hug for 10 seconds and voice our concerns afterwards. After our hug, each of us is composed enough to talk about the situation calmly and respectfully. Sometimes, the release of tension is so big that there is nothing left of the original agitation and the behavior changes. Can you think of a strategy that would work for you and your kids? If so, make sure to make the agreement official, as if you are both signing a contract. In fact, writing out the terms together and creating a signing ritual is a lesson all by itself.

2. Sit with your child after he or she has crossed a line and engage him or her in a conversation about it. You might start by telling your child what is difficult for you nowadays or what was difficult when you were a kid.

    When I asked Timon about the difficulties he might be having, he responded: "It is sometimes very difficult to listen and not to scream." We explored this topic further and at the end we both came to the conclusion that feeling frustrated is okay, as long as we know we are doing our best.

*Everybody is a genius. But, if you judge a
fish by its ability to climb a tree,
it'll spend its whole life believing that it is stupid.*

— Albert Einstein

4

Nurturing Talents

Billy Elliot, a fictional character whose story has been captured on film and in a Broadway musical, grew up in rural England and only discovered his love and talent for dance by accident when he was eleven years old. When his father sent him for boxing training, he was drawn to the ballet class that occasionally used the same gym. Initially ridiculed by his father for taking lessons in an "unmanly" discipline, Billy was not allowed to continue dancing. Yet, he secretly persisted in spite of his father's ban, and was eventually supported not only by his father, who gradually recognized and accepted Billy's talent for dancing, but also by the community.

During his audition for the Royal Ballet School in London, Billy had to describe what it feels like when he dances. As he struggled to put this experience into words, he explained that when he dances, he forgets everything else and his sorrows disappear. He compared dancing to flying like a bird and mentioned a sensation of fire and electricity in his body. Billy was eventually admitted to the Royal Ballet School and after years of training we see him in the lead role in Tchaikovsky's *Swan Lake*.

Billy's story demonstrates one of the many possible paths to discovering one's genius, embracing it and building a successful career around it that leads to self-realization and provides—in Billy's case—a stunning aesthetic experience to others, making their lives richer as a result.

Perhaps there is a piece of Billy in each of us because we all have the potential to create the greatest versions of ourselves during our lifetime. If we believe that no one is here by accident, that all people bring something valuable to the table and that each person's gifts to the world are truly remarkable and cannot be substituted by anybody else, then we are much closer to self-actualization. We all have a unique combination of talents, interests, dreams and passions that cannot be replicated. Activating and claiming them is not always easy and often requires courage, a leap of faith and dedication.

While pondering the concept of individual talent, I have come to the conclusion that there are four major steps in the process of self-actualization. The first is to discover one's unique genius; the second to embrace it; the third to develop and expand it; and the fourth is to use it creatively for the benefit of oneself and others. Each step on this road of discovery, enhancement and realization of one's unique talent can either be easy or difficult, depending on the level of genius we possess, available support (or lack thereof) we receive from family, friends and teachers, our personality and historical and geographic conditions.

Some people are lucky enough to discover their talents and passions early in life while some come to that realization later. Some never take the time or see the opportunity to find out what makes their heart sing. Listening to that voice demands that we put in the time and effort necessary to develop our potential. Sometimes we do that partially and sometimes we let those energies remain dormant for an entire lifetime. In the end, we either use our talents and passions or we find excuses to avoid that direction.

Each of us in some way probably know the feeling Billy Elliot described about loving what he was doing because we all experience something similar when we engage in our true passion and apply our talents, be it through bookkeeping, composing music, conducting research, cooking, counseling, dancing, farming, home decorating, painting, playing with children, remodeling bathrooms, swimming, teaching or writing.

All of these talents are equally important because they enrich our lives in multiple ways, creating a wonderful, multi-faceted world. It is very unfortunate that our culture places more value on certain professions and skills and diminishes others, which is usually expressed in compensation and social status. As a result, we are often conditioned or coerced to seek professions based on their social recognition and financial reward without regard for our unique talents and passions. As a result, we may end up stuck in jobs we dislike, feeling empty and lifeless inside.

There is a wonderful parable by Franz Kafka entitled "Before the Law" that shows the emptiness, meaninglessness and tragedy of a life in which a person is either afraid or too passive to follow his or her unique life path. As the story goes, a man comes to the gate leading to the law (whatever that law might be) in order to enter it. There he sees a scary-looking gatekeeper and asks him for permission to enter. The gatekeeper advises the man not to do so as there are more powerful gatekeepers inside. However, he steps aside to let the man through if the man decides to do so. But the man does not have enough courage to go inside without the gatekeeper's explicit permission, which he never obtains. The man waits futilely for years in front of the gate, hoping that the gatekeeper will change his mind. Shortly before the end of his life, the man wants to know why, in all these years, nobody else came to claim access. The gatekeeper reveals that it was impossible for any other person to walk through the gate because this path was destined for the man alone. Since the man's life is almost over, the gatekeeper can now close the gate.

So why is it not always wise to ask for permission?

Like the man from Kafka's parable, we will never know what will happen when we enter the path of self-actualization, but in order to find out, we need to try. Do we really want to end up perpetually waiting for other people's approval, for the right moment or for the courage to be served on a silver platter?

I have always been captivated by the question of how to create a deeply fulfilling, abundant and happy life, one in which I can live effortlessly, with enthusiasm, grace and poise—at least *most* of the time. This question gained intensity after my son was born. Like all parents, I felt an immediate desire for my child to be happy and fulfilled.

It is not easy to find a balance between imposing our own vision of success and happiness on our children (because we, of course, know better what is best for them) and trusting that they will find their own way. It is our job to help them discover and cultivate their special talents by introducing them to various ideas and activities, by noticing their interests and giving them opportunities to try out different things, by really listening to what they say with their words and behaviors, by encouraging them and sometimes by gently pushing them in a certain direction. But it is definitely not our job to choose their life path for them. And hopefully, we will have enough courage and faith to support them in living their dreams and passions, no matter what they are.

Since I have always considered myself quite open-minded when it comes to helping Timon explore his interests and envisioning different possibilities for his future, I was shocked to realize that I became slightly upset when he refused to continue his karate lessons. Being brutally honest with myself, I had to admit that I was not upset because he was very excited about it at first and then changed his mind. Nor was I upset about the tuition I paid for the entire month. I wasn't even upset about all the time I had spent driving him back and forth and waiting while I could have been doing something else. The thing that upset me was Timon's unwillingness to pursue *my* passion—from *my* past. Once I realized the root of my displeasure, I was able to let it go—cheerfully. I may not have a karate kid but I do have a fantastic son.

Diving Deeper

If you cannot answer all three questions below with a definitive "yes," then there is probably some inner work to be done. Let's roll up our sleeves.

1. Do you know your own talents and passions and pursue them, and do you guide your child by example, words and experience to do this as well?

2. Do you notice and support your child's interests?

3. Do you provide him or her with many opportunities to explore different topics, disciplines and skills?

4. Are you open and courageous enough to let your child experience his or her own interests, talents, passions and dreams without being stuck in your own narrow vision of how he or she should live and what he or she should pursue?

Getting Active

The nature, variety, and combination of human talents have no boundaries and no prescribed norm. Some people will be engaged in one discipline and pursue their passion in a singular and focused way from early on in life, while others will be figuring out their fascinations throughout their entire life or changing them every year. What matters is becoming aware of one's unique genius and accepting what it offers.

1. What type of genius are you? Write down situations and activities that make you feel radiant, enthusiastic, joyful and fully alive.

2. Are you always drawn to the same types of undertakings or would you rather experience a wide variety of things?

3. Do you enjoy practicing a specific skill until you master it? Or do you prefer being introduced to new ideas without the need to figure out every single detail? Is it the depth of a field, breadth of understanding or connections between the ideas that appeal to you the most? Write down your observations.

4. Set a timer for three minutes and, using your notes, describe yourself in the third person (she/he) as if you would be talking about somebody else.

5. Do you feel stuck in any area of your life? Is something holding you back? Imagine the gate and the gatekeeper from Kafka's parable. Ask yourself if you are similarly waiting for an invitation to do something for which you feel a deep calling. Is there a path that you would like to pursue but are not pursuing because you are waiting for explicit permission to do so? What fears are holding you back?

Conversation Starters to Engage Your Child

Nurturing Talents

I once saw a baby that stood on her head.
Everyone looked. "She's amazing," they said.
I wondered what talent I had to call mine,
And then once I found it, how would it shine?

Could I jump really high or run really far?
Maybe I'm ready to drive a new car.
Or singing is something I think I do well,
Along with the stories I always can tell.

Maybe my talent is building a tower
Or drawing a beautiful, colorful flower.
I'm always quite good finding shells at the beach.
I might know enough to get hired to teach.

With talents and skills you might call amazing,
I could even get better with some friendly praising.
Enjoying the challenge to pass the next test,
I can't wait to discover what I can do best.

Getting Active Together

1. What type of genius is your child? Ask the same questions you asked yourself as they relate to your child, modifying them where appropriate.

2. What challenges do you see your child facing, such as not being able to switch easily from one activity to another or needing longer transitions between different segments of the day or not being able to focus on one endeavor for a longer period of time? Does your child insist that he or she can do things, which you know they cannot? Does he or she avoid certain activities on a consistent basis? What genius could hide behind them?

3. Ask your child to write down their dreams and wishes and a list of what they think it would take to achieve those visions.

Good health is not the absence of symptoms;
it is the presence of peace.

— Neale Donald Walsh

5

EMBRACING HEALTH

When I noticed one day that Timon had been pilfering the sweets that I thought were securely out of his sight in the kitchen cabinet and was hiding them in the laundry basket so he could access them when I was not looking, I realized that my somewhat restrictive approach to food choices was not working.

If I could have it my way, there would be no junk food available to children—and no other types of junk for that matter, such as super hero movies, Barbie dolls or toy guns. No junk food that is setting up our kids for obesity, diabetes and other health problems, not to mention the images inflating ideals of hyper masculinity, glorifying violence and ratcheting up the desire to obsess about over-sexualized standards of beauty.

But I cannot have it my way because we are bombarded with all kinds of junk every single day from all directions. It is ingrained way too deep in our culture and there is too much money being made by food and entertainment industries. No matter how frustrated I become with our mainstream consumer culture and how much I want to keep it away from my home and family, I cannot ignore the fact that it is everywhere and its messages are pervasive. Like the matrix, it is inescapable and I am confronted with it every time I take Timon to school, a birthday party or a store.

Choosing from all of these foods, TV shows, films and toys makes it possible that any location can turn into a battleground between parents and children. Is it better if these conflicts escalate because parents set limits on what their children can consume or is it better if there are no struggles because kids get what they want? Do parents just give in too easily because they already indulge in similar types of junk? Is there a middle ground, and if so, where––and how––do we draw the line?

When I came to realize that my initial approach to selecting food and entertainment was becoming a touchstone for Timon to assert his own sense of autonomy, I chose to back down considerably. Logically, the more restrictive I became the stronger his resistance grew.

I still refuse to buy sweets full of chemicals and hydrogenated fats. I will not purchase toy guns, Avenger paraphernalia or things of that nature. But now––as much as it pains me to admit it––I will make the occasional trip to MacDonald's or a bakery and once in a while we all indulge in cheap pizza and ice-cream for dinner. And, as much as I would like to limit Timon's TV intake to PBS programs for kids and feel-good movies, I am now open to other films and series available online. In fact, during our latest expedition to a toy store––at the mall no less––I even purchased a toy bow with arrows, as opposed to––as Timon put it––"another toy that is supposed to make me smarter."

I have come to think that maybe it is not as much about controlling every bite on the plate and every scene on the screen, but rather about offering an appropriate variety of available options, discussing the consequences of consuming junk food and aggressive images, making smart choices as fun as possible, and at some point, letting go of the desire to control every step.

That's the hard part!

As many parents discover while juggling their different responsibilities and tasks day in and day out, the emotional attachment to food is often stronger than any intellectual understanding of nutrition. Being overly concerned—or sometimes obsessed—with food and/or calories is something countless women know quite intimately. It's no secret that struggling with food choices seems to be a bigger challenge for women. It only gets compounded when their children are always aggressively campaigning for snacks, snacks and yet more snacks.

It should come as no surprise then that we make misguided food choices. We do so for a variety of reasons, including an unfamiliarity with the basics of nutrition, a lack of awareness of the body's needs, an absence of appreciation for our body, cultural conditioning, that never-ending, all-pervasive messaging from the mainstream food industry, a desire—conscious or not—to use food to numb emotional pain or emptiness, financial stress and in some areas—known as food deserts—an unavailability of nutritious and affordable foods.

The truth is, we always have the choice to treat our body as a temple or a trashcan. We can respect it or abuse it. We can love it or hate it. We can be grateful for all it does or we can insult it. Either way, our body and health will *always* reflect the choices we make.

Everyone feels pain and emptiness at some point in their life. It can originate from a variety of sources and its history varies with each person. Using food—or other substances and addictions—to numb ourselves emotionally is a familiar method many of us have chosen to escape the discomfort of feeling empty, depressed or powerless—you name it.

When we reach for food—or drugs, alcohol, compulsive shopping, overworking, gambling or any other suspect activity—we are able to temporarily forget and numb the pain we experience. In the long run, however, we will feel less alive and multiply our pain. The inner imbalance is *always* revealed through the imbalance on the outside.

So what is the solution? There are probably many. One that appeals to me and has been helping me through many situations is presence and acceptance. Presence is the awareness of the moment with all its nuances. Acceptance is first the ability not to resist the painful feeling by distracting ourselves from it through food or other things. Then it is the courage to invite the feeling and experience it fully, as painful as it might be. Once we do this, the feeling will start to dissolve and we will appear on the other side of it with the realization that our soul is much greater than the discomfort or anguish we experienced. And in our essence, we are complete, beautiful, and invincible.

In my own struggles with physical and emotional well-being, I have come to see health as an abundance of life force freely flowing through every cell of my body—vitality, radiance and strength of my physical body, as well as inner harmony, peace and joy.

During my journey toward holistic well-being, I have learned the importance of energetic balance and what a unity of body and mind really means. This has occurred only since I started paying attention to the foods I was eating. I used to indulge in hamburgers, French fries and colored sugary drinks, even though these foods made me feel heavy and depleted of energy. Occasionally, I chose a variety of healthy alternatives and when I did, I felt fantastic, both physically and emotionally. Not only was I energized by the victory of choosing an apple over a donut, but my body also responded to that selection in a wonderful way, although not right on the spot.

Yet, most of the time I kept making the same unhealthy choices. As a parent with daily routines of school, work and maintaining a household, I could compensate for my lack of time for myself with a gallon of ice cream or soothe my ever-expanding to-do list with a bag of potato chips.

Making the transition to mindful and healthful eating came gradually. I slowly came to realize that every time I was emotionally out of balance my mind would demand instant relief, often in the form of donuts, potato chips or cheesecake.

But I paid a price for that. I knew I had to change. I learned that a unity of mind and body can support cravings for foods that work *for* and not against my body. I came to realize that my body always knew which foods would support my optimal health and if I really listened to its messages by being present and aware, I probably could have avoided the health challenges I was facing. I learned to believe in the body's miraculous ability to heal if we only learn to listen to its messages, develop a positive relationship to it and do not sabotage it by destructive thoughts, emotions, and habits.

So what do donuts, toy guns and Barbie dolls have in common?

At the end of the day it is all about becoming aware of what we really do—and why. If I consume a gallon of ice cream it is definitely not about enjoying a dessert. If my friend buys a car she cannot afford, it is not about having a safe vehicle. And if my other friend spends all of his free time at work at the expense of his health and family, then it is not about his work ethic. It is about escaping from the discomfort of the present moment.

There is no escaping yourself or your bad habits. Your best friend is a healthy body and you can show your ultimate love for yourself— and your child—by taking care of it.

Diving Deeper

When we are (metaphorically) asleep, we keep living on autopilot and perpetuate the destructive habits and convenience-based choices by numbing ourselves with junky food and entertainment. So how can we wake up? Maybe these questions will help us to take the first step:

1. Are you aware of how you make your food choices? Are they based on habit, convenience and the desire to escape the present moment or on thoughtful educated choices, a concern for well-being, and reverence for your body?

2. What are your food choices teaching your child?

3. Are you too restrictive or not restrictive enough regarding the food and entertainment that your family consumes? How does your child react to these restrictions or lack thereof?

4. How can you convey to him or her probable outcomes of consuming junk food and aggressive images? How can you make smarter choices for your child as fun as possible?

5. How can you translate the concept of holistic health into your child's understanding of the world and encourage him or her to embrace it?

Getting Active

Here are some strategies that have worked for my family and me:

1. Try to catch yourself whenever you are about to do something that feels out of balance. (Remember my gallon of ice cream?) By the way, that also applies to screaming and cursing.

   STEP 1: Practice presence. Notice what is happening in your body. Take mental note of your feelings. Where do they reside? If these feeling had a form, would it be a person, an animal or a monster? How exactly would it look?

STEP 2: Practice acceptance. Do not try to resist the feeling. Welcome it and ask what it is trying to tell you. What would it want from you? Accept whatever answers come.

2. Identify your numbing strategies, the things you do to escape the present moment when it starts feeling uncomfortable or painful. Is it one particular thing or several? Imagine how your life and your body will look like in five years if you continue engaging in your particular escape strategy on regular basis. What impact will this have on your child? Describe that prospect. Now, take a different piece of paper and describe the opposite: your life in five years if you stop engaging in that undesirable habit *now*. It's your life—make your choices wisely.

3. Unplug your TV for one week or if possible, put it in the garage. Make a deal with your family that there will be no TV for seven days and set an attractive prize for everybody, yourself included. You may have to include computer games and mindless Internet surfing in the agreement—whatever it takes to get your family away from the screen. Instead, go for a walk, play board games, go bicycle riding, explore your house and the backyard with a flashlight when it's dark, tell stories, draw pictures, or anything else that does not include sitting in front of a screen. See what happens. I bet it will be a really good week.

Conversation Starters to Engage Your Child

Embracing Health

I like to feel healthy and bouncy and good.
That's why I eat all the things that I should:
Lots of veggies and brown rice and fruits that I like.
And when I'm done eating I'm riding my bike.

I know lots of ways to grow up big and strong,
Like drinking clean water all the day long.
And brushing my teeth well each morning and night
Will make them stay healthy and cleaner and white.

When I go for a walk or a run in the sun,
A cap and some sunscreen can make it more fun.
That's because I feel happy to know I can play
All day in the sunshine protected that way.

Good health is a blessing for young and for old;
It makes life much better, or so I've been told.
So say no to junk food and watching TV.
You have one special body; I hope you agree.

Getting Active Together

1. Whenever your child gets angry, sad or disappointed, ask him or her similar questions as you asked yourself, e.g. Where do these feelings reside? If these feeling had a form, would it be a person, an animal or a monster? How exactly would it look? You can, of course, add more questions, e.g. What do these feelings taste, smell and look like? What color are they? Encourage your child to draw. You can engage in a role-play conversation between the feeling and your child.

2. Watch the Portuguese animation series *Nutri Ventures: The Quest for Seven Kingdoms* (available free on YouTube), in which a villain keeps people under control by hiding all natural foods from them and forcing them to eat "Genex 100"—food manufactured by him and devoid of any real nutritional value. A group of kids embarks on a quest to reclaim natural foods and travels through seven kingdoms (Dairy, Meat and Eggs, Fish and See Food, Legumes, Grains, Vegetables and Fruits) to discover the nutritional value of fresh and minimally processed foods. The kids also venture into the deceiving Kingdom of Sugar, where people have been hypnotized to crave sweets and admire their fancy colors, shapes, and textures. As a result, they are unable to see them for the repelling and disgusting substance they really are. Discuss the film with your child.

3. Design a menu for one day with your child. Look up the nutritional values for each meal and write down or draw how these foods impact your body, e.g. if you have milk (dairy, almond, or coconut) you can write "calcium" and draw strong bones next to it.

Cultivate the habit of being grateful for
every good thing that comes to you,
and to give thanks continuously. And because all
things have contributed to your advancement, you
should include all things in your gratitude.

— Ralph Waldo Emerson

6

CULTIVATING GRATITUDE

In an old Native American tale, a grandfather tells his grandson that there are two wolves in every person's heart, always fighting against each other. The first wolf lives a life predicated by fear, full of negative feelings such as anger, insecurity, aggression, doubt, jealousy, regret and hatred. The other wolf's life is motivated by love and an array of positive emotions, such as confidence, compassion, kindness, trust, hope, joy and peace.

"Which wolf wins the fight?" the grandson asked his grandfather.

"The one you decide to feed," the grandfather replied.

Whether it's fear or love that influences our emotional life and subsequent behavior, we can choose a life based on discouragement and negativity or a path that leads to positivity and empowerment. But just as we cannot think two different thoughts at the same time, it is also impossible to look at life simultaneously through opposing angles, such as insecurity and confidence, aggression and compassion or doubt and trust.

Similarly, in our relationships with our children we also can choose between automatic reactions and mindful parenting, between soulless discipline and a deep connection. Instead of remaining stuck in our own way of perceiving the world we can try our best to see the world through our child's eyes. In each of these three oppositions, the first choice seems much easier, at least at first. It's a no-brainer to opt for the prevalent "Super Nanny" approach instead of slowing down and considering a bigger picture.

Solving what's needed in the moment often takes precedence over what approach might be best in the long run. And how we perceive the world as an adult usually wins out over the perception of a child. But why? Is it because the second option in all three cases requires more effort, open-mindedness and self-discipline, leading to a more holistic vision of parenting? Like in the Native American tale, the better question might be: which wolf will we decide to feed?

How we approach various elements in our daily lives, such as events, people, relationships, obligations or leisure, can be quite revealing. Is our dominant motivation positive or negative? For example, the way we look at other people when we casually watch them pass by might be quite telling. Do we observe them like thoughts during meditation, without attachment and judgment, or do we stick mental labels on them? Do we mainly perceive what is "strange and different" in them or do we realize at that very moment that they are just like us—with an entire array of fears, vulnerabilities, hopes and dreams? Doesn't our way of observing also tell us something about ourselves?

During a recent trip overseas, I realized that while observing people at the airport—either rushing desperately to get to the right gate on time or sitting comfortably in the food area—I was noticing all of the negative things about them and taking mental notes of what I automatically perceived to be their deficiencies. The negative list of imperfections that my fellow travelers spurred in me went on and on. Suddenly, it struck me that I was actively seeking or even worse—creating—negativity. Why was I doing that?

Scientific research shows that our natural tendency is to focus on the negative more than the positive. One possible explanation is that this happens as a remnant of our evolutionary development. We notice the threat and the unexpected as a matter of survival, something that began thousands of years ago. In fact, the human brain processes negative and positive information and stimuli in two different hemispheres and stores corresponding memories differently. Not only are we more likely to notice the negative sooner and faster, but we also tend to remember criticism longer and in greater detail than praise. Losing $100 impacts us more that gaining $100 and we are more likely to pay attention if there is something undesirable, adverse or potentially harmful involved. We perceive people voicing criticism as smarter than people expressing approval.

But that day at the airport, I made a conscious decision to work against these impulses and to actively look for something positive in every passerby. I was able to find likable, attractive and pleasant features, behaviors and attitudes in everyone I observed. As a result of this conscious choice, everything became more fun.

Gratitude follows the same principle. There are so many things in our lives—even during the most difficult times—for which we can be grateful, but because we usually take them for granted we do not allow ourselves to really appreciate what we have. Instead, we often focus on what we lack or things that do not go as we would like.

Simply waking up in the morning and seeing the new day as a gift with its potential for miracles instead of dreading to get up and proceed with the routine of everyday life requires an immense shift in attitude. If we focus on being grateful for our life then it is impossible to feel unhappy.

Sometimes, of course, that is easier said than done. During my pregnancy and after my son was born, I suffered from severe depression and thought that my life was falling apart. The experience was not new to me because I had struggled with depression before—to the point of being suicidal in my twenties. What was surprising, however, was the fact that it caught up with me after so many years of emotional balance and peace of mind.

Although I have been quite successful professionally, I was emotionally devastated right after Timon was born, not just due to the serotonin imbalance in my brain but also because I realized that the position I had just accepted—and moved across the country to begin—was not a good match for me, even though it might have been considered quite wonderful for other people. So when my son was six weeks old, I gave up that job and thought it meant the end of my career, one I had studied and worked for most of my adult life.

I moved to a place where I did not want to be because my husband had a job there and felt that our marriage was crumbling. I was incredibly lonely, far away from my family and friends, not knowing anyone in the area and failing at first to find like-minded people. When my husband's company suddenly started downsizing, I became terrified that we wouldn't be able to pay for the house we had just purchased. All in all, I saw no way out from a situation seemingly out of my control.

The only happy moments occurred when my son was awake and I could interact with him. I loved holding him in my arms, feeding him and looking at his toothless smile. When he slept, I sat on the floor and cried. Sometimes, I just stared at the empty walls of my new home, my tormented mind going round in circles, telling me I would never be able to continue my career, that my husband would lose his job and that we would be kicked out of our home, leaving me and the love of my life (my husband) broken apart.

Yet, as an educated woman living in the US, I was extremely privileged and exceptionally lucky. I did not endure mass rapes in Congo. I did not witness my family massacred in Syria; nor did I have to work 16 hours per day under the constant threat of fire in a Bangladeshi sweatshop, earning 13 cents per hour, and risking being burned alive.

Of course I did not see how privileged and lucky I was back then because being depressed and focusing on my own misery made my world very tiny. It is like having a huge beautiful tapestry of life that spreads over miles, rich in color and texture, and zooming in on a tiny little piece of that tapestry, half an inch small, that shows something that looks like a bent over, little ugly goblin. By practicing gratitude and focusing on all of the things we have and take for granted, we expand our view of the tapestry of life and suddenly we realize that the little goblin is not that ugly after all as we see him bending to help another creature get up off the ground. Seeing the bigger picture and looking at things in perspective helps cultivate gratitude.

In order to come out of my despair six years ago, I slowly reached out for help, from family, friends and strangers. I read countless inspirational books; started appreciating things around me; decided what I really wanted and visualized and affirmed them all.

It was a very challenging time. Taking anti-depressants was the easy part. What was really difficult was practicing the mental and emotional self-discipline I imposed on myself in order to get better— in spite of the persistent and almost inescapable pain that is not physical, but seems to envelop one's entire being; in spite of the lack of vitality to engage in any, even most basic, activities; and in spite of the dwindling desire to continue.

"This too shall pass."

I wrote that quote in lipstick on my bathroom mirror and looked at it every day, working hard on not letting my mind scare me into a panic and not giving in to despair. I trained myself to become an optimist and to be grateful for everything. At first, it was an immense struggle because I automatically fell back into my old thinking and emotional patterns.

But eventually, step-by-step, things started shifting. After one year, I had my dream job, moved to Southern California, where I always wanted to live, sold the house, renewed a loving relationship with my husband and was happier than ever before.

So why is it important to feed the right animal?

The changes I experienced did not come overnight. They took a full year of nourishing the wolf of love and keeping the other one at bay—through dedicated effort, focus and determination.

One of the most empowering questions I asked myself during these unhappy and dark moments was: "If this was happening for my greatest good, what are the best things that could come out of that situation?" Amidst desperation, panic attacks and loneliness, I tried very hard to come up with a list of these good things, such as becoming wiser and stronger, strengthening the relationship with my husband, getting my dream job and finding a way to move to Southern California. Not only was I able to reach these goals; I experienced many unexpected wonderful things along the way, especially the power of gratitude, the power of intention and reaching out for help. But it still amazes me how much we can change and turn our life around so relatively fast—if we use all of the mental and spiritual tools we have available.

I have learned that gratitude is much more than simply saying, "thank you." It is a profound and multilayered process of learning to feel on a very deep level so that it truly comes from the heart and overflows into the entire body and beyond. But practicing gratitude is not only about feeling grateful when we get what we want. The real challenge is to feel it even when we *don't*.

"You get what you get and you don't throw a fit."

In other words, gratitude can be embraced as a way of life, but we must embrace it with sincere intention. Creating intentions makes us much more aware of what we truly need and want. As we go through the day running errands, driving kids to school and going to work or meetings, it is valuable to think for a minute *before* embarking on an activity of how we would like it to go and to visualize the perfect outcome. Setting positive intentions not only for the year, month or week, but also for individual sections of each day, can help us stay present as we mindfully accomplish what we have to get done. Sometimes, it might be wise to set an intention that focuses not only on *doing* but also on *being*. Instead of forcing ourselves to complete a task that we have been postponing forever, we can set an intention of being focused and disciplined. How and who we decide to *be* in the world may be more important than what we decide to *do*.

Diving Deeper

While we often are motivated by a particular attitude or feeling by default, it is important to remember that we can deliberately choose it. Not only do we have a choice to approach every situation either from a place of a negative or positive emotion/attitude, but we can also look at past events and choose our story about them to be either crippling or inspiring. In this context, it might be worth noticing how we approach life:

1. Which wolf do you regularly feed? Which one is behind your everyday reactions to people and events?

2. Do you acknowledge people, experiences, and things you am grateful for? Do you talk about them to your child? Are you truly able to feel the gratitude on a deeper level as opposed to just mindlessly saying "thank you"?

3. Are there any situations or relationships in your life that could benefit from changing your underlying attitude or emotion, from setting a specific intention or from asking for help?

Getting Active

These activities can help us remember the importance of consciously cultivating positive attitudes and emotions, embracing gratitude as an approach to life and sharing these practices with our children.

1. Start by taking notice of what happens first thing in the morning when you take a shower or wash your face: the warm running water, the scent of the soap, a soft bathroom rug under your feet or that wonderful face looking back at you in the mirror. Take a moment to really feel the experience. This will open up the possibility for gratitude on a deeper level.

2. Set up additional rituals in your house or neighborhood that will give you—and your children—the chance to express gratitude on a regular basis. For example, tending a garden or reading about how one's favorite food is grown can be a powerful reminder of the wonderful things we have in our lives and often take for granted.

3. Think about your day and identify a few things you were *doing* and list them (e.g. working on a project, driving, playing with your child, etc.). Now identify how/what/who you were *being* during each of these activities (e.g. I was an unfocused procrastinator while working on a project; impatience personified while driving; or absent-minded compulsive email-checker while playing with my child). Were you being the person you want to be—or not? Identify what quality you would like to personify for the rest of the day and do it. No, don't *do* it. *Be it!*

Conversation Starters to Engage Your Child

Cultivating Gratitude

Each morning I wake up so thankful to know
That my family is with me wherever I go.
From breakfast till dinner and all in between,
I know that I'm lucky to have such a team.

I'm also so grateful the sky is so blue.
Look out through the window and you'll see it, too.
The swallow is gracefully stretching its wing;
Flowers bloom everywhere, thankful it's spring.

Whatever the season, there's much to enjoy,
Like good comfy shoes and my favorite toy.
From playing with insects to watching the moon,
Each day is so full, and it's ending too soon.

I wish for more hours than just twenty-four;
There's so much to do and I want to do more.
Be thankful; be grateful; I'm sure you'll agree
That life is fantastic for you and for me.

Getting Active Together

1. Ask your child before bedtime about the five best things he or she experienced during the day. You can probably quite easily point out to your child how fortunate he or she is and why we can be grateful for what we have.

2. Sometimes I engage in a role play with my son that is quite amusing for both of us. I pretend to be Timon and he pretends to be me. This introduces the distinction between doing and being to your child. You may also discover new things about yourself!

3. Donating money for a good cause or giving it to a homeless person is something you can do with your child. Giving to people who have less than we do can definitely help acknowledge how much we really have, in addition to maybe making the day for someone else.

4. While most people feel uplifted by reaching out to someone in need, many people don't like to ask for help because they perceive it—consciously or not—as a sign of weakness or a burden on the other person. Yet, we all need help from time to time and we should not stop the flow of generous energy by insisting that we manage by ourselves what in reality may be quite beyond our ability at a given moment.

    Discuss with your child whether or not he or she withholds asking for help when it is really needed. Make a list of those times and how your child might better ask for help next time. This same exercise might easily apply to you, too!

Do what you can, with what you have, where you are.

— Theodore Roosevelt

7

LEARNING TO YIELD

For someone who has always considered it essential to be in control of everything, becoming comfortable with a certain lack of control—which I was reminded of recently during a family trip to Yosemite—can be a most liberating experience.

On the second day of our five-day adventure, we came very close to packing our bags and returning home. Not because we did not like our cabin or the spectacular views or because Timon got a mild cold. We almost left this wonderful paradise because my husband and I had a difference of opinion—to put it mildly—about how we should spend our time there. Each of us, including Timon, had a very different vision of what constitutes a perfect vacation.

My husband, Önder, wanted us to go on several all-day mountain hikes.

"Why would a father do that to a six-year-old kid?" I thought.

Timon was mesmerized collecting dried branches and sticks from the meadow.

"Why can't we do something more exciting?"

Önder and I shared that sentiment, but only to a point. Personally, I wanted to sit quietly in a remote place and connect to the spirit of nature.

"Really?" my down-to-earth husband asked. "Connect to what, exactly?"

Does it sound familiar, anyone?

Initially, none of us seemed inclined to back down from what we thought we should be doing but then, as we grew more enchanted by the beauty of our surroundings, we started going with the flow. We stopped imposing our individual preferences on the other: where to go, what to see and do, and just let ourselves follow opportunities as they presented themselves.

As a result, we ended up doing all the things each of us wanted, without resistance, confrontation or defiance. Instead, we eased through our days with a spirit of adaptation and understanding. We ended up enjoying our trip immensely because each of us was able to give up some of the control we thought we needed.

Opportunities like this are available to us every day, even far away from the amazing confines of a place like Yosemite. However, we usually do not take advantage of them because we are so focused on how we think the opportunities should present themselves rather than simply letting some of them happen. But being so sure of when and how we think we are going to be happy and enjoy life may very well deprive us of the ability to actually do so in a real, spontaneous way.

That does not mean that we should not dedicate our energy to getting what we want or reaching our goals. On the contrary, we can do whatever is in our power to get where we want to go, but at some point, we just need to let go and trust that we have done everything we could to receive what we want and the rest is up to the universe.

Being desperately attached to an outcome is like proclaiming: "I cannot be happy in any other way than I imagined for myself." That could become a self-fulfilling prophecy.

I like to plan everything carefully, have things under control and constantly keep my eye on the big picture. Unexpected events can throw me off balance. I am like a professional chess player who plans all the moves ahead of time and does not want to be surprised.

But since life *is* surprising––over and over again––and does not seem to play exclusively by my rules, I have decided that it would be beneficial for everyone if I were to approach unanticipated situations and events in a welcoming way, instead of becoming uptight and irritated.

While learning to approach the unforeseen with ease and grace, I came across two ancient Taoist parables that perfectly depicted the state of mind I strived to achieve when confronted with the unexpected. The first one tells of a man who fell into a wild river leading to a high and rocky waterfall. People who witnessed the accident cried in despair because they were convinced that the man would not survive. So imagine their shock when some time later they saw the man walking up stream next to the river, wet and cold, but otherwise unharmed. They immediately asked him how he survived.

"I accommodated myself to the river," he began. "I did not resist it and did not try to control it, but rather I allowed it to shape me. I immersed myself in the raging water and came out with it. I let the waterfall take me down and floated up with the river."

This parable teaches us not to argue with life, but instead to cooperate with it. We need to take whatever it is that life throws at us, acknowledge it for what it is, learn from it and find a way to turn it to our advantage. As Jon Kabat-Zinn so aptly titled his book on meditation, "Wherever you go, there you are." It's hard to argue with such a statement.

Whether we like the place we are in or not, that's where we are and the sooner we acknowledge and accept it, the better. During some of my most difficult times, I have developed a mantra that I repeat to myself.

"That's how it is."

This mantra has helped me acknowledge the situation for what it was and from that place I could move to finding ways of getting myself out of whatever hole I was in at the time. Without it, by remaining stuck in my own wheels, I could not move beyond the circumstances that were fencing me in.

"That's how it is."

As soon as I spoke the mantra I felt relief and liberation. Like the man in the parable, I stopped resisting and trying to control the river and immersed myself in the raging water. Instead of drowning, I opened my mind and heart and floated up with the river.

When we go through life being inflexible, the currents may very well swallow us up. What we might consider wise—insisting we are right, demanding to be accommodated, fighting for control or suppressing what we feel—can be replaced by letting go, becoming accommodating, acknowledging our emotions and letting them pass through us on the way to forgiveness. As we see in the parable, giving in is more beneficial and teaches us to stop struggling against life and to look for alternatives that bring more peace and contentment.

So how does one survive falling into a wild river?

Although we can't fully control our lives, we all can decide how we want to respond to challenges as we work with what life gives us. At any given moment, we have all we need to take the first step towards the outcome we desire, be it becoming the parent we want to be, improving our health and energy level, achieving financial independence or any other goal we might have. Seeing opportunities and potential for the extraordinary in unpleasant situations requires self-discipline at first until it becomes a habit. It also requires yielding and a practice of mindfulness.

Mindfulness is paying close attention to one's thoughts and emotions as they arise in the present moment, without judging them as right or wrong and just observing them. As we do that, preferably in a quiet place—but not necessarily in a lotus pose or twisted like a pretzel—we will notice that the self that observes the thoughts and emotions is the real self—vast, peaceful and wise—and that the thoughts and emotions are just that—thoughts and emotions—that will pass and change like clouds in the sky. From that place, we can choose our reactions. We can decide to think a different thought, let the emotion dissolve through acceptance or a mindful action. This is the real power—the control over one's mind—not the control over other people or external circumstances.

While the first parable teaches us to yield and find our advantage through mindfulness and wisdom, a second tale shows us that things are often not the way they appear at first.

An old farmer was unable to till his fields because his horse ran away. The neighbors came to express their sympathy.

"Such bad luck," they said.

"We'll see," the farmer replied.

The next day, the horse came back with three wild horses. Upon hearing the news, the neighbors came to congratulate the farmer.

"Such good luck!" they said.

"We'll see," the farmer replied.

On the following day, the farmer's son tried to ride one of the wild horses and fell off, breaking his leg. The neighbors came again and conveyed their empathy.

"Such bad luck," they said.

"We'll see," the farmer replied.

On the fourth day, the army came to the village to draft all eligible young men. The farmer's son was spared because he had a broken leg. The neighbors came again to express their joy over the farmer's good fortune.

"We'll see," the farmer replied.

The wise farmer knew that situations we perceive as undesirable can also become our greatest gifts. Similarly, the events we welcome with delight might not turn out as we think. It can be life changing when we learn to see alternate possibilities, so that when life seems not to be turning out to our advantage we can still be open to its gifts.

Diving Deeper

Things are not always as they appear. Rather than becoming overly attached to outcomes, we might consider accepting that sometimes the only thing we can control is our response to a situation. That approach can save us from unnecessary agitation. How you respond to these questions can reveal a lot about where you stand in this regard.

1. How does your child see you reacting when things do not go as planned?

2. What is he or she learning from my reactions?

3. Do you look for opportunities in challenging life situations?

4. Do you try to give a positive spin to situations you do not necessarily like?

5. Do you reframe these situations and articulate the potential benefit for your child?

6. Do you take what life throws at you, acknowledge it and work with the energy to turn the situation to the highest good—for yourself and others?

Getting Active

Just for fun, try these simple activities. Maybe one day they will help you retain your sanity when you are on the brink of losing it. Teaching mindfulness to your child might be challenging at first, but it will definitely help *you* learn it. Don't we sometimes teach the things we, ourselves, need to learn most?

1. Practice mindfulness. Find a comfortable place and sit quietly without distractions for at least ten minutes. Notice your thoughts and/or emotions. Try to perceive that there is a self that observes and a self that is being observed within you. Identify as much as you can with the observing self that is much greater than your thoughts, emotions and reactions. Can you sense the stillness, vast space and deep wisdom within your observing self? Does it feel like deep peace and tranquility?

    Release all judgment of what the right thoughts and emotions should be in favor of impartially noticing what is happening on physical, emotional and cognitive levels. There is no "right" or "wrong" here, only what is. Try to be at peace with whatever comes up, even if it is "What am I even doing practicing this stupid exercise if I could be doing something with *real* results?" By the way, *real* results will come if you stick with practicing mindfulness every day, when suddenly, as if out of the blue, you will start feeling generally more peaceful, joyful and happy, flowing effortlessly through life.

2. Develop a mantra that will help you through a challenging part of each day. Maybe while getting your child ready for school you can try singing "What a beautiful day we have." If you are having trouble getting yourself to the gym, keep saying, "With every step I am becoming fitter, healthier and more beautiful," etc.

3. Identify something in your life that is not going exactly as you wish. It can be small or big. Instead of resisting it, try to accept it for now but don't confuse acceptance with giving up. Try saying *mindfully* (really concentrating on the words) "That's how it is." See if you feel a sense of relief.

Conversation Starters to Engage Your Child

Learning to Yield

I went out to play till it started to rain.
I could have been mad, or I could have complained.
But when I found cool stuff to do in my room,
I skipped the bad feelings and banished the gloom.

Later, when I went to watch some TV,
The TV was broken, so I drew a tree.
Then, looking in closets for glitter and glue,
All I could find was a sock and a shoe.

On days just like this, when things don't go your way,
You have a big choice: you can whine or just say,
"I don't care if it rains or I can't find some glue.
I can always find something much better to do!"

Learning to change and to grow can be fun,
But sometimes it's easier said than it's done.
I'm planning to try out so many new things;
I'm taking some chances to see what life brings.

Getting Active Together

1. Sit together with your child and focus on the present moment. Ask your child to identify all of the sounds you both can hear, i.e., cars, dripping water, air-conditioning, neighbors, etc. Ask your child to notice and describe the colors, textures and shapes of things in your environment. *Are the clouds really white? What does a peach truly feel like?* Ask him or her to engage the senses of smell and taste. *How does the morning air smell? Can you describe the taste of a banana?*

2. Sit together again and encourage your child to pay close attention to everything that is happening inside his or her body, thoughts and emotions. Ask questions like: Is there any discomfort or tightness in your body? How do your feet feel on the floor? What exactly are you thinking? Are you happy, sad, angry or slightly irritated? What other emotions do you feel?

3. Ask your child to look around the room and remember as many details as possible. Then, ask your child to close his or her eyes. Ask questions about the details of the surroundings and see how many will be correct. You can do this anywhere. It might be particularly useful in a waiting area.

What you do makes a difference, and you have to decide what kind of difference you want to make.

— Jane Goodall

8

RESPECTING LIFE

"Timon, it's time for our adventure."

"Where are we going today, Mom?"

"It's a surprise and I bet you will really like it."

I grabbed my bag, checking for sunglasses, water bottles and anti-bacterial wipes. Maybe I should take that large bottle of hand sanitizer, just to be on the safe side. I decided that it definitely wouldn't hurt to have it in the car.

We were ready for our great adventure—a trip to a landfill, a place I would have never thought of visiting, much less taking my son along, if not for one of my colleagues mentioning that during her last visit there she had seen a dead giraffe on top of a pile of trash.

That definitely got my attention. I arranged a private tour to become more educated about the facility and the level of bio-hazard risk involved in its operation.

Surprise! We were the only visitors.

Timon didn't find the visit as exciting as I expected, in spite of being surrounded by countless enormous, noisy trash trucks as we entered the site—but it was very educational nevertheless. We learned about all the technicalities of trash disposal and landfill operation, including the brilliant idea of powering the facility with the methane gas created by the decomposing trash.

When we returned home, I made a firm commitment to significantly reduce my trash output. I became quite meticulous about sorting recyclables and reusing whatever I could. Actually, it was Timon who demanded that we put all plastic bottles, cans and glass in separate bins and take them to a recycling center. He especially liked the five-cent deposit per bottle he could collect and put into his piggy bank.

Our landfill visit reminded me of the time I lived in Germany, where throwing out trash is a very intricate and carefully regulated endeavor, with separate, color coded bins for unsoiled paper (paper coated or bonded with other materials is not included), plastic and compound materials (one needs to know the exact specifications of what should and should not land there), non-returnable glass bottles and containers separated by colors, biological waste, old clothes and shoes, batteries and electronics. And then there is a single bin for whatever garbage remains

All of this is regarded quite seriously, so it better not even cross your mind to put a glass jar in the same container with its metal lid or to throw away used Kleenex in the bin designated for clean paper. We may shrug or giggle at the obsessive-compulsive nature of these efforts, but Germany has consistently reduced its yearly trash output.

So what's the lesson in this? It is worth considering how others take care of their environment and why they choose to act the way they do. At the same time, it may be quite enlightening to ask ourselves why we choose to do things as we do—especially since there are alternatives. Finally, we could try to adopt what seems worthwhile, like the general concern for our environment and the human footprint on our ecosystems.

It should be safe to assume that all parents want their children and grandchildren to inhabit a planet with clean, breathable air and drinkable water, one that does not deplete its natural resources, expand its ozone layer and continually wipe out more and more animal and plant species from the face of the Earth. In spite of our best wishes, we are on a fast track to create the type of planet we do *not* want for our kids.

Like many other parents, I have taken my child to a planetarium and marveled at the wonder of our planet. Peering into the blackness of our infinite universe, we pick out the Earth, a dark blue, iridescent sparkling ball of light with white swirls of water vapor shimmering above its surface—the only known planet in the solar system capable of sustaining life. Yet amidst the limitless universe and among countless galaxies, where distances are measured in astounding and mindboggling numbers, we too often just hang around, living our lives rather aimlessly at face value, rather than being in a state of perpetual awe and appreciation.

The Gaia hypothesis in the fields of natural sciences (in Greek mythology, Gaia—the Earth—was personified as the mother of all living things) states that the Earth is a living, breathing planet, where everything is interrelated and operating as one complex, interacting and self-regulating system. When any sphere of the system goes out of balance, i.e., atmospheric, geological, chemical or biological, the other spheres adjust accordingly to reestablish equilibrium. This is what should occur in a system that is inherently meant to sustain *all* forms of life, not just human beings. This concept inspires me to reconsider the interconnectedness of life and my own relationship to our planet. It has also forced me to take responsibility for any of my actions that can affect our habitat.

In the film *Avatar*, the inhabitants of Pandora worship their planet as a life-giving mother figure. This connects them mentally and physically to every organism living on their planet. While the concept of Earth as a mother figure is not new, viewing the interconnectedness and interdependence of all earth systems can hopefully lead us to address our current environmental predicament and increase our awareness of the potential for global catastrophe.

It all could start with an inquisitive attitude about the activities we engage in every day and a series of simple questions. Am I aware that the electricity that flows when I turn on the light comes (most likely) from fossil fuels—extraction and transport of which has destructive influence on the environment? Am I interested in finding out how the remnants of animals on my plate were treated before they landed there? Do I even want to know what toxic dyes have been used to treat the clothes I am wearing? Were the vegetables I am about to prepare for lunch genetically modified and treated with pesticides that might have long-term harmful effects on my family's health? How many trees are being cut down each year to produce paper for my needs? Is my old computer being shipped to Nigeria or Pakistan, where children will extract highly toxic materials, poisoning them and the environment in the process? How about all of the plastic—some from Timon's old broken toy—that ends up at the bottom of the ocean among tons of garbage, leaking toxic chemicals into this ecosystem?

So what can we learn by visiting a landfill?

I suspect we don't really want to know the answers because of what that would mean for us and our way of living. I know that I am guilty of many sins against the environment, like leaving lights on when I don't have to, letting the water run while brushing my teeth, forgetting to use reusable bags at the grocery store, wasting food products because I bought too many, throwing old batteries in the trash and buying too many pairs of shoes.

But at least I am asking myself how I can modify my actions on a consistent basis and encourage my son to choose behaviors that are environmentally and socially conscious. I'm on my way to doing better. If each of us can develop an affinity for nature and a sense of responsibility for our environment, then we could have cleaner air and water, less trash and toxic waste hovering just below the surface of the earth and in the oceans, not as many harmful chemicals in our food and homes and more healthy forests around the globe. In other words, we could have better lives and a brighter future. It's really up to us.

Diving Deeper

As parents, we must consider how our actions impact the future of our children. That should spark a deeper reflection about the ways in which we personally treat our planet.

1. How can we translate the desire to live on a clean, sustainable, and flourishing planet into practical actions?

2. Do your choices reflect this wish?

3. How do you teach your child to have high regard for our planet and its resources and act accordingly?

4. Albert Einstein once said: "Our task must be to free ourselves by widening our circle of compassion to embrace all living creatures and the whole of nature and its beauty." Does this resonate with you? If so, how can you convey its message to your child?

Getting Active

Implanting the idea of taking responsibility for our Earth can start at any age and place. It can involve anything we enjoy doing or are interested in trying out. This task is actually quite easy because children's natural curiosity makes them open to exploration. It is us grown-ups who often need a kick in the rear end to become more active and involved.

1. Choose one item in your household (a piece of clothing, cleaning solutions, coffee, notebook—really anything) and find out how this product was made and transported. How did its production impact the environment, and how could it affect the environment after disposal? Keep asking these questions as you go shopping.

2. Take one action today that is environmentally and/or socially conscious and notice how you feel about it. Does it make a difference for you? It could be as small as turning off the water when you brush your teeth—or bigger.

Conversation Starters to Engage Your Child

Respecting Life

My parents call nature a delicate thing;
So did my teacher the first day of spring.
We're supposed to respect it, but what does that mean?
Should I protect it and keep it all green?

The creatures and flowers, my mother explained,
Are meant to be treasured and quite well maintained.
That means we enjoy them but never abuse;
The nature around us is not ours to lose.

The grass and the trees and the birds in the shade
Must all be respected, just as they're displayed.
So don't pick the flowers—just leave them alone.
Don't scare wild rabbits—you're a guest in their home!

I want to know more about bugs and the bears,
But the woods aren't just ours—they really are theirs.
We have to share carefully, living as one.
We're all part of nature, right under the sun.

Getting Active Together

1. Include your child in a project that involves learning more about our impact on the environment and/or a concern for our planet, such as visiting a landfill, setting up a compost bin, collecting recyclables and taking them to the recycling center, finding out what happens with these recyclables afterwards or participating in a river or beach cleanup.

2. Explore different aspects of nature together with your child. You can engage in planting vegetables or a tree, watching and identifying birds, looking for animal tracks, finding star constellations, following an ant trail or making a tree leaf collage. And on a rainy day, you can go to a children's science museum, watch a film about animals or explore geography.

3. Take a fruit (or any other food item) that your child likes and find out where it comes from and how it got from there to your kitchen. Ask your child to draw an outline of the fruit's journey.

It is not our differences that divide us.
It is our inability to recognize, accept,
and celebrate those differences.

— Audre Lorde

9

CELEBRATING DIVERSITY

"**T**hat one looks like a giant mouse with a piece of cheese in its mouth," I said to Timon.

"Yes, I see it," he replied. "And look, there is a whale with elephant ears."

Lying on the grass in the park, we had a delightful time describing the shapes of clouds, which soon led to identifying different shades of colors, like various whites in clouds or greens in the trees and just goofing around.

"Can you think of four things that have no colors?" I asked.

"Air, uh glass, water and uh, I don't know," Timon said.

"Can you think of one more?"

I was trying to push him a little further although I couldn't come up with the fourth one myself.

"I know," Timon suddenly said, breaking our silence. "People have no colors."

On the one hand, I thought his response was brilliant. It was fresh and unspoiled by society's need to label people according to race or ethnicity or any of the other categories we impose on each other. But I also felt that we cannot negate our social reality that, for the most part, is not color blind or ignorant of ethnicity, gender, religion, class, etc. I thought about how these labels—fraught with stereotypes and expectations—have real consequences for people, but Timon does not know that yet. For him, people have no colors and are treated equally.

Laying under a tree on a perfect balmy day, I wasn't about to start puncturing my son's bubble of contentment. But I became a little apprehensive, thinking ahead to the day when I would have to begin discussing this whole topic with him in detail.

Where will I even start? How will I explain racial profiling, hate crimes, social privilege and abject poverty? I can't simply leave the discussions to his teachers in school or his friends on the playground. When the time is right, I must be responsible—to Timon and myself—for explaining how our society works and whether or not it is fair and progressive.

What are these categories anyway—race, ethnicity, gender, religion or social class? Social sciences and humanities refer to them as being socially constructed, a concept that might seem confusing at first but does help us to understand the social dynamics among various groups. It can change how we perceive and approach other people, and even more decisively influence how we define our own identity.

But what does "socially constructed" actually mean? People have different skin pigmentation; they come from different parts of the world, identify as male or female, follow an organized religion (or not) and have various education and income levels. Those are the facts, so what are we constructing about them as a society?

Socially constructed means that there is a set of expectations and assumptions attached to people based on the label they have been given—very often mistakenly. For example, expecting that all people who identify with a particular religion are dangerous and suspicious or that all women are not good in math. The second aspect of the social construction concept is the fact that the categories we impose on each other are often arbitrary. Why do we divide people by skin color, for example, and not by eye color or height? Couldn't we just divide people according to those who embrace differences and those who do not?

My friend Melissa told me about an incident she witnessed in a grocery store while she was shopping with her three-year-old. A young man seemingly in his thirties, clean and well dressed, came up to her out of the blue and insulted her and her son with a bunch of racial slurs. And then he just turned around and proceeded with his shopping as if nothing had happened. The man was white, or as Melissa described him, rather pinkish. Her son reported that he was the color of a pig. By the way, Melissa and her son are a beautiful caramel shade of brown.

Melissa was so shaken by the man's vitriol that she froze and was not able to say a word. Several other shoppers stopped in their tracks, staring at her and the man, and without a sound, they continued with their shopping. A minute later, the entire spectacle was over, but for Melissa and her little boy, the entire day had been altered.

I was outraged when Melissa told me this story and worried about how her little boy might be affected by the situation, how it might impact his self-esteem and ability to trust people in the future.

I had to ask myself what I would have done if I had been a fellow shopper who happened to be in that aisle when the man approached Melissa. I can't say that I know for sure—none of us can until we are facing such a moment—but I certainly hope I would have challenged the man in a calm and definitive way—and even more so if my son were with me. Even if what I would say would not be terribly effective, reacting is what really matters, to make a stand and defend what is right, as a matter of my own principles and as a lesson for my son.

Being an academic person, I did my due diligence and found research showing that a majority of people will not say anything in a situation like this, usually because they feel intimidated and uncomfortable or just don't know how to react. But we must speak up! We have to support people who are verbally attacked. Open disapproval and condemnation might isolate a racist like that man. If he's called out on his actions, it may even make him less likely to voice those thoughts publicly in the future.

It's a question of doing the right thing. Of course it's what we should do for anyone in a situation like Melissa and her son, but it can also provide the person standing up for others with a sense of deep satisfaction.

"Do what's easy and you will have a difficult life," the famous saying begins. "Do what's difficult and you will have an easy life."

This is an especially important lesson for our children and it can begin when they observe even a very small moment of civil courage and acts of kindness towards other people. I cannot think of a more powerful lesson we can teach our children than standing up for what we believe is right. And this, in turn, might help them make the right decision and speak up if they should ever face or witness bullying or any other type of discrimination.

I am white––or creamy beige according to my make-up bottle–– which makes me less likely to be exposed to bigotry, and I have never been discriminated against because of my race. So I don't know how my friend Melissa really felt in that grocery store and how many times she has been offended and discriminated against because of the way she looks. I can only imagine how horrible this experience was for her.

But many of us know what it's like when other people try to define who we are—based on their stereotypes or just plain ignorance. And our children will eventually encounter these kinds of situations. Therefore, knowing who we are, what we stand for and what we will and will not tolerate—simply defining ourselves for ourselves and others—is essential and can become a very empowering and inspiring way to live.

Once in a while, I still hear this innocent question, prompted by how my native accent affects my English. I don't consider it racist, but these questions can't help but come across as thoughtless:

"So when are you going *back home*?" I am asked.

And then, depending on my mood, I reply.

"Well, I will be *in my home* in one hour."

"No, I meant to *your country*," comes the reply.

"Ah, but this *is* my country as much as it is yours."

That usually creates an awkward moment of silence before I either explain my origins, change the subject or take my leave.

As a woman, however, I can say with certainty that I have been treated on multiple occasions like someone perceived to be less competent, somewhat dependent or simply not an equal person because of my gender, as if I were just an extension of my (male) husband.

This has happened to most of the women I know. When my friend Tamara went to buy a car and was asked by the charming car dealer if she maybe would prefer to come back with her boyfriend, she left with no intention of ever returning. One beautiful Saturday morning, I opened the door of our home to face two attractive men who wanted to convert my family to their version of God. Not surprisingly, they politely requested to speak with the head of the household. When I asked innocently what had led them to think that it wasn't me, they quickly demurred and retreated down my front steps.

So how can watching the clouds transform your thinking?

These situations used to upset me but what's the point of getting all worked up? If I'm feeling relaxed when they occur, I can even find them amusing. I will ask kindly for clarification, explain why their particular sentence or question might be misdirected and offensive, and try to suggest an alternative, if possible and appropriate. If they seem to mean well, I may even search for a way to compliment and encourage their potential progress.

Stereotyping and prejudice are not the exclusive domain of racists and extremists. We all have our preconceptions and biases—which is a wise thing to acknowledge. This point is made very clear at the Museum of Tolerance in Los Angeles. There are two doors to enter the first exhibit room—one is for "prejudiced" and the other for "unprejudiced" visitors. Most visitors, including myself, want to enter through the "unprejudiced" door. We are visiting the Museum of Tolerance so we must be open-minded and unbiased, right? Wrong. The "unprejudiced" door is locked and cannot be opened by anyone, precisely because nobody is unbiased. How could we not be if we all view the world through *our* own identity and experiences?

Naturally, we all have blind spots. We view people according to the subjective model of the world that we believe is right. And that perspective is determined by our identity, cultural norms, traditions, religion, socio-economic status, gender, geographic location, etc. While our similarities might bring us comfort, we learn and grow through encounters with differences. To embrace the diversity and see it as a resource is one of the many gifts we can give to our children and also a wonderful contribution to the world.

Diving Deeper

Instead of stigmatizing people, pigeonholing them and reducing them to their markers of "difference" (such as skin tone, head covering, religious symbols, etc.) we could use these opportunities to learn more about these people's perspectives, cultures, fears and hopes. We could focus on what we share—our humanity—and embrace our differences as an expression of the delightful variety of life. Don't we all want a more peaceful and inclusive world for our children? So ask yourself:

1. Which parts of your identity are most important to you and why?

2. What meanings do you attach to them? For example, what does being a woman or having a particular ethnic background, etc. mean for you?

3. Is there a group of people that you consider "different" in some ways from the group you identify with? How are you *constructing* the difference, that is, what meanings do you attach to being of a certain race, ethnicity, gender, religion, class, etc.?

4. Do these meanings come from the media, personal experiences, common stereotypes, or somebody else's opinions?

5. What would you do if you were witnessing the incident in the grocery store, in which Melissa was insulted with racial slurs? What would you say?

6. Do you know what you stand for, what you will and will not tolerate?

Getting Active

These activities might help you see yourself and other people in quite a different light:

1. Next time you watch a film or news broadcast, ask yourself how gender, race, ethnicity, religion, etc. is *constructed* there? If you would be asked to form an opinion about a particular group of people (men, women, people of various religious and ethnic backgrounds, etc.) based only on what was presented in that film or broadcast, what would that opinion be? Does it feel biased or objective?

2. When you meet a new person, try to be as open as you can as to who they might be. Try to encounter them with a completely open mind, a tabula rasa. Try to find out more about their background, identity, hopes, and dreams.

3. Take one or more questions from the "Diving Deeper" section and write about it for five minutes.

Conversation Starters to Engage Your Child

Celebrating Diversity

I know lots of people who act differently;
Some are like you, and some are like me.
Some are so quiet, and some are real loud,
While some may feel shy and some are so proud.

Some kids have dark skin while others are light;
Some like to sing songs and some like to write.
Some eat just veggies while others go hunt,
And some read their books from the back to the front!

We sing and we dance and we strum a guitar,
And celebrate just how special we are!
So that's how we roll; we keep no one away.
No one gets left out, in class or at play.

We all are so different in specialized ways.
It makes life exciting, with no boring days.
From our cares and our prayers to our family name,
By being so different, we're all still the same!.

Getting Active Together

1. Lakeshore Learning carries "People Colors Crayons" that come in all shades and nuances of human skin color, but there are also similar collections by other companies. It might be worth purchasing a set and drawing family, friends and neighbors.

2. It is fascinating to see that diverse cultures from around the world have different versions of similar stories. The differences in the stories derive from geographical locations, the origins of the tale, and cultural norms, but the underlying plot can be quite similar. There is, for example, a Cinderella story on almost every continent with numerous versions from Egypt, Korea, Vietnam, China, India, Cambodia, Germany, Italy, France, and Mexico to name just a few. Borrowing some of the versions from a library and reading them with your child could be fascinating. Apart from a particular version of femininity in the Cinderella tale that might not be most desirable for girls to absorb, discussing the differences with your child could be quite thought-provoking.

3. Explore a world map with your child. Talk about different countries, traditions, geography, climate, plants, and animals. What natural resources do people in different parts of the world have available? What are they lacking? How could their customs and traditions be shaped by the geography, climate, and environment? Why do they eat particular foods? What kinds of houses and dwellings do they have?

Embracing our vulnerabilities is risky but not nearly as dangerous as giving up on love and belonging and joy— the experiences that make us the most vulnerable.

— Brené Brown

10

REMEMBERING TO LOVE

"How could you do that?" I shouted at Timon. "Haven't I told you hundreds of times not to touch my computer?"

For a brief moment, I stood silently, stricken with terror and then I started running like a mad woman around the house, screaming with desperation.

"Timon, how could delete everything from my computer?" I shrieked, almost afraid to even go near him. "This can't be true. I can't believe you would do this!"

Obviously, I was oblivious to my own parenting philosophy, the one that supports using humor and finding ways to lighten up when thing get stressful.

Five minutes ago, it has been a blissful Saturday morning. Timon was at my desk, drawing and gluing paper. I was curled up on the couch with a cup of tea, thoroughly at peace, enjoying the chance to read a book I was eager to finish. It was a perfect day. I am not sure how long I was immersed in my book but when I emerged Timon was still working on his art project—at least that's what I thought until I approached my desk and saw my laptop screen.

"Are you sure you want to permanently delete all of these items?"

Before I could do or say anything, Timon clicked the "yes" button, setting off the quiet metallic sound of the trash bin emptying on my desktop, effectively saying goodbye forever to several very important documents, job and personal life related, products of hundreds of hours of dedication and creativity that I had for some reason never backed up.

I felt as if the end of the world has just arrived. I didn't even think. I just lashed out. I was probably screaming for more than a minute, prancing about in a rage before realizing how angry I was. Timon was still sitting at my desk not saying anything.

Finally, I stopped yelling and stood staring at the screen, as if maybe if I stared hard enough at it my files would return from the grave.

"Do you still love me?" Timon asked quietly.

His little voice instantly brought me back to reality. I was still shocked and very angry and did not try to hide it. Of course I loved Timon—profoundly and unconditionally—but in my response to him, I had a choice to be cruel or loving. I could have responded in the spirit of love or not.

"I love you and I always will," I said, squatting by his side, "no matter what you do."

I felt a sense of relief because I had been able to stop myself from saying something cruel while completely hooked on my anger and out of touch with my real self. Who was I angry at more—myself for foolishly not backing up my files and not putting away my laptop or Timon for touching my computer without permission and deleting my documents?

A few minutes later, I explained to Timon the damage he had caused by deleting my files and how that demonstrated why he was not permitted to use my computer without asking. I also apologized for screaming at him and explained why I had become so angry. Timon acknowledged that what he did was wrong and explained that he had gotten bored with drawing. He apologized and promised not to do anything on my computer ever again without my explicit permission. We agreed that he would make it up by helping me clean my office for one hour every day for a week instead of going to play with his friends.

Later on, when I tried to analyze the situation from Timon's perspective, I reflected in general terms on what happens when children don't listen or follow the rules, act out or have a tantrum, and how we react as parents when our kids' behavior is out of line.

So why did Timon delete my files? On that fateful Saturday morning, why didn't he follow the rule of not touching my laptop without my permission? There are many possible explanations. He is a very curious and energetic child who cannot focus for too long on one activity. Naturally, he got bored with drawing and gluing. Several days before, I had made up fake documents on my laptop and let him drag them around. He loved that metallic sound of emptying the recycle bin so much that I probably made thirty fake documents for him to delete. Why wouldn't he want to pursue that entertaining activity on his own? He probably did not even remember the rule of not taking my computer without asking when he recalled how much he had enjoyed deleting files. He followed his inner logic, the desire to experiment and the path of anticipated fun. It made perfect sense.

But I could view Timon's behavior as a challenge to my authority, a malicious act with clear disregard for family rules. I did not have to talk to him or say that I was sorry for screaming. I could have just sent him to his room and imposed some disciplinary measures without communicating with him or explaining anything. I am glad I did not because on some level it would have pushed us apart emotionally––even for a short period of time––but still, who knows what consequences that could have? If these types of situations would occur more often, the emotional distance could grow over the years. Instead, I believe that my reaction, aside from the initial screaming, which is not an example worth emulating, established more understanding and a deeper connection.

It is important to consider the entire context when judging a child's behavior. I am not a purely permissive parent, encouraging or excusing unacceptable behavior or relieving my child from responsibility for his actions. Rather, I am advocating looking at things from different perspectives and taking all possible explanations into account—not only the ones that align with our mood or perspective at any given moment. Maybe it is worth considering that when children act out or don't listen, it's not because they want to challenge or provoke us or because they are mean or selfish. There might be very logical—and not so negative—reasons for it. If we are open to that possibility and willing to look at these behaviors—not with an eye of a disciplinarian but with more love and compassion—we could build more trust and deeper connections with our children.

For example, it used to drive me crazy that, when I was picking Timon up from school, he invariably wanted to show me all of the activities he did that day and demonstrate new acrobatic tricks on the monkey bars—while all I wanted was to go home. When bedtime approached, he would run away and expect me to chase him as an extension of his playtime. The list goes on. Eventually, I came to realize that his postponing tactics are not an expression of defiance but that it is difficult for him to instantly shift from one activity to another. Many children, in fact, need longer periods of transition between activities. Acknowledging this and considering Timon's delaying strategies in that light has made it much easier for me to make the necessary adjustments and helped create much more pleasant days. Accepting that our children will not always behave as we wish is not easy. It requires empathy, patience and a healthy dose of self-discipline. The result, however, is very desirable.

So how can deleting computer files lead to a greater understanding of human nature?

On that memorable Saturday morning, I was reminded that words can be used in an empowering and loving way or as a means of discharging uncomfortable or strong emotions. I continually must remind myself of the power of words to heal or wound.

This connects logically to the basic principles of nonviolent communication, developed by Marshall B. Rosenberg in the 1960s, which has been very helpful in my interactions with people. I have not mastered them yet, but what I have learned so far has been transformational in the way I approach people and how they respond. The underlying assumption is that all people share universal basic needs (e.g. the need to be understood, respected, loved or to feel significant in some way, as well as the need for personal freedom and autonomy) and that these needs are being met—or not—in our relationships.

Nonviolent communication is based on four steps: (1) acknowledging our (usually negative) feelings generated by interactions with a particular individual, (2) identifying what exactly in the other person's words or behavior triggered these feelings, (3) expressing these feelings honestly without judging, criticizing, blaming the person or assuming what his or her intentions were, and (4) making a straightforward request to the other person to change that behavior.

Since we interpret what other people say or do through our own lens, our understanding of their intentions is often a carbon copy of our personal motives and preferences, at least to some degree. Therefore, it might be wise not to assume or judge what the other person intends to do or accomplish. Instead, stating our neutral observation about the thing that made us feel uncomfortable and articulating how we feel about it is a much more effective way of communicating. People cannot really become defensive about an objective observation, but they usually will be defensive if they are blamed or judged.

An honest expression of our feelings and our truths requires the courage to be vulnerable, but as I discovered in my own journey, it is not possible to engage in any kind of meaningful relationship without that courage. What I mean by being vulnerable is letting go of the fear of being judged, not accepted or validated in some way, and just be who we truly are. We often tend to cover up our vulnerabilities through an entire array of tactics, such as creating emotional distance, aggression, sarcasm, making things up, exaggerating, coming up with excuses, etc., because we are so afraid of being emotionally wounded. Of course, we might get hurt and disappointed if we reveal our true self, but that's the risk we all have to take to develop deep, meaningful, and significant connections with people.

How do the principles of nonviolent communication apply to parenting? The first step is to try to see the situation, in which our child misbehaves, in an objective way, also considering a possible child's perspective and to refrain from judging it as bad or good. The second step is to ask ourselves what need the child might be fulfilling by behaving in this particular way and clarify and/or validate the child's feelings, which does not mean that we are approving of the behavior. The third step involves conveying to the child the implications and impact of that behavior on everyone involved in a non-judgmental way. Any of the tactics we sometimes use such as blaming, shaming, forcing, punishing, isolating, etc. will be met with resistance, defiance, or fear and will—sooner or later—cause a disconnect between ourselves and our children. The fourth step is making a suggestion for repairing the situation and avoiding similar acts in the future, not as a command or demand, but rather as a mutual agreement.

When we can accomplish even some of these principles, we put ourselves—and those closest to us—in a position to love and be loved.

On that blissful Saturday morning when Timon couldn't help himself from destroying my computer files, I used those principles— once I came to my senses, of course—to achieve the desired results. There was no resistance, defiance, submission or fear involved, which in my view contributes to more trusting and richer relationships.

Showing respect even if our kids do something they were not supposed to do, trying to understand their motivations and reasons, validating their feelings, yet holding them accountable as well as setting limits and enforcing them is something I am continually perfecting.

Diving Deeper

When thinking about your relationships, ask yourself the following questions:

1. What communication strategies do you use in conflict or difficult situations?

2. Do you ask honestly for what you need?

3. Do you set limits with things that make you feel uncomfortable?

4. Do you manipulate people to do what you want? Do you threaten or put people down?

5. Are you generally submissive, passive aggressive or aggressive?

6. If you identified any of the negative communication strategies, how long have you been using these strategies? How do you think you learned them in the first place?

7. What would it take for you to change them into something positive?

8. Do you let yourself be vulnerable in relationships with people? Are you able to let go of the fear of being judged, not accepted or validated in some way and just be who you truly are? Do you cover your vulnerabilities by emotional distance, aggression, sarcasm, making things up, exaggerating or coming up with excuses?

Getting Active

Based on your reflections from the previous sections, come up with different strategies and action steps that will help you be a more effective communicator with your child and others.

1. Create one positive communication strategy that you could use in place of a negative one. Anticipate situations in which you might tend to use the negative tactic and make a resolution to use the positive one instead next time.

2. Choose a recent situation, in which your child did not behave as you wished he or she had. Write a list of all probable motivations and reasons why he or she might have acted this way. Identify different possible interpretations of the situation.

3. Review the steps of a nonviolent communication strategy in the text and write down the things you could have said in the recent situation in which your child misbehaved. Focus on stating what happened in an objective way. Describe observable facts, asking if your child's behavior was motivated by a particular need. If so,

name that need in your question. Validate the feelings. Explain the impact of the situation on you and/or the surroundings and agree mutually on the steps that your child will take to correct what happened.

Conversation Starters to Engage Your Child

Remembering to Love

Inside my own bed I feel cozy and snug.
Each day I wake up to a kiss and a hug.
My parents, they always remember to say,
"Good morning, dear sunshine! We love you today."

But sometimes I wonder, in case I do bad,
Will my parents still love me and make me so glad?
Of course they will, silly; they'll love you the same,
If you're up or you're down or not quite on your game.

If you're ever in doubt or just feeling unsure,
Like wondering if love can be constant and pure
In spite of a harsh word or maybe a shout,
Just never forget what love's all about.

One thing is for certain: when push comes to shove,
There's really no question when it comes to love.
Your family and friends are there for you, too,
To make sure you know that their love is all true.

Getting Active Together

1. Make a list of things that constitute violent communication for you and your child, e.g. screaming, saying hurtful things, refusing to talk, etc. Make a contract, in which you both commit yourselves not to resort to these strategies. Come up with a list of alternative ways of communicating when you are upset. Post the list on the fridge or any other prominent place. (Doing this with your partner or spouse might not be a bad idea, either).

2. Take a situation either from your own life, something you both observed, or borrow from a book, film or cartoon. Together with your child, analyze this situation from the points of view of everyone involved. Try to reconstruct all possible motivations, reasons, feelings, etc.

3. Together with your child, choose a few sentences and take turns saying them with different emotions, as if you would be angry, silly, grateful, happy, annoyed, etc. Have fun role-playing! You can always use this activity in real life to restate something that was said with anger or irritation in a more constructive and positive way.

4. Practice with your child saying or restating everything in a more positive way. I actually did this recently when I caught myself saying, "This stupid Internet is not working again!" Oops! I meant to say, "Our wonderful Internet is not cooperating yet."

There are only two ways to live your life.
One is as though nothing is a miracle.
The other is as though everything is a miracle.

— Albert Einstein

11

BELIEVING IN MIRACLES

I enjoy my one-hour commute to work. Whenever I mention this, I get strange looks from my friends and colleagues.

"You must be crazy," is the usual. "That freeway is a nightmare."

During rush hour it certainly is, but I'm lucky. I'm on the road at five a.m. and on my way home in the afternoon before the bad traffic begins. That leaves me two hours a day of uninterrupted thinking or a nice long dose of non-commercial public radio.

Several months ago on my way to work, I nearly had a serious accident. As I was enjoying the smooth flow of traffic, a truck in front of me suddenly slowed down, forcing me to slam on my brakes. Thankfully, I avoided a crash but the car I saw in the rear view mirror was quickly zeroing in on me. For a second, I thought this was the end. I froze with my hands on the wheel, arms outstretched, my back and head crunched down into the seat, anticipating the terrible impact. At the very last second, the driver behind me veered into the next lane, missing my car by inches.

My pulse was racing; my thoughts were jumping around like crazy rabbits and it took me quite some time to calm down and process what had just happened. Could it really be so sudden and easy to lose one's life or be seriously injured? That was the first time I had ever been confronted with those real possibilities, except for years ago when my ex-boyfriend published a lovely story about me, apart from the fact that it ended with my tragic death. Although I'm still not sure if I should be flattered for being immortalized in literature or disturbed by the way his story ends, I do know that it's a piece of fiction, which clearly distinguishes it from that very real morning on the freeway when I barely avoided a serious accident.

Was that a miracle, a coincidence or just another typical near miss on the freeway? Could the laws of physics explain it or were supernatural powers at work? My grandmother would say that I have a guardian angel, and I want to believe her. Wouldn't that make life easier and more manageable? It would be like having a cozy blanket available whenever I get cold feet.

When I was about six years old, my grandfather taught me a short unconventional prayer that gave me a feeling of security and reassurance that everything in life will turn out fine. I think he came up with this prayer on his own because I have never heard it anywhere else. Every time I was scared or alone in my room at night, I repeated this prayer over and over again until the fear disappeared and I felt peaceful and happy. Unfortunately, I cannot remember the words of this prayer, but I definitely recall the warm feelings it gave me.

Faith is a complex issue—or very simple—depending on how we look at it. Most of us inherit our religious beliefs from our parents and we either accept those doctrines and continue their tradition, or we come to question their significance for our own lives, which sometimes leads to rebellion as we redefine it, reject it completely or choose something else entirely. While organized religion is the right path for some, others prefer a non-denominational, spiritual approach.

Yet it has always seemed to me that regardless of our faith, most of us connect at least a part of ourselves with some miraculous energy, be it God, the universe, a higher self or whatever other name we may ascribe to what we believe in. Once we are old enough to reflect on more abstract principles, we accept or choose a particular faith and worldview—be it more scientific, philosophical or religious—that aligns with the core of who we are as human beings.

We can go around convincing everybody, including ourselves, that our religion is the right one but it's easy to forget that our passion may not ring a bell with everyone. While arguing about the details of the scriptures, prophets, afterlife or an appropriate way to live according to our creed, we can easily forget the things that really matter: love, compassion and kindness. And at the end of the day, when we are confronted with a tragedy or something that seems too difficult to handle alone, we hope for a miracle. When alternatives fail, we often turn to God—either the one we have believed in all along or the one we previously rejected.

When we become helpless and desperate, confronted with our own mortality or in danger of losing a person dear to our heart, we either believe in miracles, the power of prayer and a caring God—or we deeply wish we did—at least one of those.

I briefly knew a wonderful man, Greg, a CEO of a big company, whose daughter was in critical condition after an accident. The doctors did all they could to save her life, but it was not clear for several days if she would live. Out of his determination to see his daughter get better, Greg—who was not a religious person—called every single person he had ever known and asked them to say a prayer for his daughter. I found Greg's story extremely touching and awe-inspiring. While he will never know for sure if it was the prayers, the doctors or something else that helped his daughter recover, Greg definitely came to recognize the power of believing in miracles.

My grandmother was deeply religious and prayed every day for my good fortune. This was one way she expressed her love for me.

I do have a wonderful life and generally have been very lucky and blessed in spite of some difficult times. Of course, I will never know if my grandmother's prayers contributed to my good fortune, but I want to believe that they have. There are so many things that cannot be explained by natural or scientific laws, things we don't understand and things we deeply desire to be true, especially during the really tough moments, so why not to choose to believe in miracles? I do, in spite of my skeptical and rebellious nature, and it makes my life that much more fascinating, a bit easier and less scary.

Believing in miracles is easier for little children because when they are still young they see Santa Clause, the tooth fairy and various magical creatures as real. And why not instill that belief in their minds, at least for a little while? Don't miracles usually happen to people who expect them, anyway?

One of my favorite scenes in *The Matrix* is Neo's visit to the Oracle. When Neo asks the Oracle if he can trust her, she says, "The bad news is there's no way you can really know whether I'm here to help you or not, so it's really up to you. You just have to make up your own damned mind to either accept what I'm going to tell you or reject it." That's what a belief in miracles is really all about. We are free to choose to believe—or not.

For me, miracles are not necessarily supernatural interventions, but rather everyday coincidences, lucky occurrences, intuition or a gut feeling—all of which I have been able to experience in many seemingly *miraculous* ways. I am still puzzled and stunned by some of these occurrences; especially ones that seemed so strange and serendipitous at the time that I had to write them down.

I also have some *miraculous* abilities, which include a knack for finding or meeting exactly the right people at the right time, an instant gut feeling about people's negative thoughts and intentions and the ability to always secure the perfect parking spot.

Last December, Timon't teacher described to me how he fervently defended the existence of Santa Claus to a little girl who said that Santa does not exist because one cannot see him. I was actually quite stunned to hear Timon's defense.

"If you cannot see something," he said, "it doesn't mean that it doesn't exist."

I think we can all agree that what is invisible to the human eye can also be more powerful than the things we can see. While it has taken me time to trust my intuition and come to this point, now that I have, life seems a little bit more effortless.

Diving Deeper

Considering that our personal beliefs span an entire spectrum from religion through philosophy to science, our individual interpretations and outlook on life can vary considerably. With that in mind, we might ponder some of those messages and ethical principles, as well as the power of believing in miracles. These questions are intended to help you begin that process.

1. What role do the values of love, kindness and compassion play in your life?

2. Do you want your child to think of you, when he or she hears the words—love, kindness and compassion?

3. One way of recognizing a person's true character is to see how he or she treats the people he or she does not need. How do you treat people you don't "need" or people who do not have any power over you?

4. What miracles in your life are you grateful for?

Getting Active

You might approach these activities with a grain of salt—or not. Either way, who said we need to be serious all the time?

1. How do you define miracles?

2. What miracles have you experienced in your life? The birth of your child might be a good place to start.

3. Describe any coincidences and lucky occurrences you can recall. How can you explain them?

4. Write down any examples of when you chose to follow your intuition or a gut feeling. What was the outcome in each case?

5. What are some of your *miraculous* abilities?

Conversation Starters to Engage Your Child

Believing in Miracles

I feel safe in my bed all alone in the night.
I imagine I'm guarded with sparkling light.
A silver beam circling, creating a shield
Of angels and fairies and energy fields.

I can always connect with this magical power,
Protecting me daily, each minute and hour,
Providing a safe port in rough, stormy seas,
Offering a nest way up high in the trees.

But one thing's essential, a thing you must do:
I call it believing in what you make true.
Each one of us has it, this feeling inside
That miracles happen, that magic can guide.

Believing in wonders when others say no
Can make you feel stronger and help you just go.
The rules are real simple; just hold them so dear:
Think happy thoughts and choose hope over fear.

Getting Active Together

1. Select a few children's stories centered on miracles and read and discuss them with your child.

2. Visit a park or playground together and pretend to be detectives, observing people of all ages to see if you can spot any miracles happening right there in front of you.

3. See if your son or daughter can miraculously locate a parking spot when you need one.

*I learned that courage was not the absence
of fear, but the triumph over it.
The brave man is not he who does not feel
afraid, but he who conquers that fear.*

— Nelson Mandela

12

LETTING GO OF FEAR

"**S**pider! Aaah!"

Timon jumped up from his seat, his eyes wide open, as we were sitting around the breakfast table in our new kitchen.

"Get it away!" he demanded.

We had just moved from an apartment into a house where the spiders in residence were not about to move out just because we had moved in. But since these long-legged, small-bodied creatures are not harmful to humans, I decided for the time being to leave them alone. After all, they adore the taste of ants, another species that seemed to feel quite at ease in our new home.

By this time, Timon couldn't decide whether he should run out of the room or crawl up on top of the table. I knew he was afraid of spiders because he welcomed every one he saw with a fearful scream. But since I was unwilling to spray poison all over the house in a perpetual war against our new housemates, I instigated what I hoped would be the perfect solution. Actually I borrowed the idea from my friend, Celine.

The situation called for intense mediation between Timon and the spider. I looked at the graceful little bug and then at Timon, who was frozen, waiting to see what I would do.

"This is my friend Johnny," I said quite seriously, "and he has come to spend the morning with us."

I will never forget the expression on Timon's face. First, he appeared quite puzzled and then really amused. Consequently, we engaged in a somewhat philosophical conversation about the nature of friendship. From then on, Timon was no longer afraid of the long-legged spiders—or the ants—and we all lived together happily ever after.

That became our lesson in letting go of fear and befriending it.

This can be applied most easily to relatively silly little anxieties like being afraid of spiders, mice or darkness. But there are other fears that are more difficult to make friends with and they inevitably surface when we are about to leave our comfort zone and do something risky, like public speaking, asking our boss for a raise, quitting a boring job without the immediate prospect of a new one or following our biggest dream. Since feeling fear in any of these situations can just become an obstacle to getting what we ultimately want, can't we decide at some point to put our fear aside and take a leap of faith?

We can feel the fear, in fact we should probably be aware of it as a safeguard against doing something totally stupid, but as Susan Jeffers' suggested in her seminal book, we should "Feel the Fear and Do It Anyway." Pushing through our fears, which can often turn out to be exaggerated, can lead us to great rewards.

As parents, we often share an array of fears pertaining to our children's future. We might worry that they won't eventually make it to college or that they won't be successful, whatever that word might mean for us. We might fret about their ability to make friends in a new school, whether their strong-willed nature will soften with time, whether we spent enough quality time together or if we have inflicted any deep psychological wounds by yelling at them from time to time when we are frustrated, tired and stressed. It is inevitable for parents to ask these questions, but as we look into our own hearts for answers, we should remember that we are probably doing the best we can and lightening up a bit might be a good solution.

But what do we do when we feel deeply helpless and vulnerable, when the fear that emerges from real events becomes terrifying or even paralyzing? I am referring to the existential, life-threatening fears that shake us to the core, often incited by current affairs in a world that seems to be growing more and more violent and out of control. With mass shootings, police antics and environmental tragedies occurring regularly, how can we contain our fears?

There is no question that people do horrible things to their fellow human beings and hearing about them makes us feel nauseous, helpless, outraged and more fearful. We push the thoughts away that this could happen to us because they are too terrifying and painful. But they keep returning, especially when we hear about yet another shooting, another hatred-ridden individual and another case of contempt for human life and dignity. In these moments, I want to cuddle with my son longer, hug my husband tighter, be more compassionate and understanding towards other family members and even strangers and gentler with myself. The fear of what I cannot control makes me want to treasure, even more, every minute of my life.

Fear is an emotion that arises as a response to a real or perceived threat. It causes changes to brain chemistry, activates various biological systems and induces physiological responses in the body. We all know that unless we are faced with imminent danger where the fight-or-flight response can be lifesaving, fear is counter-productive, an often paralyzing feeling that prevents us from thinking clearly and enjoying life.

Unless we use the fear as a propelling force to contribute to a tangible change in the world (e.g. organizing for stricter gun control laws, helping victims of a disaster, etc.), we might be better off when we let go of fear—by whatever means we can. Actually, taking an action in these two areas might be the way to go. Nothing scares fear away faster than taking action.

Several years ago, I completed a state-certified training for sexual assault counselors. Thereafter, I worked as a volunteer for a rape crisis hotline and provided support at the hospital during forensic exams for victims of rape, sexually abused children and their families. Through that experience, I learned about many repulsive details of human behavior. I had nightmares, became more cautious when dealing with strangers and felt powerless because I could provide only limited help. Yet I realized that just being there and caring was important. For most people, suffering in solitude makes everything worse and sharing the experience with a compassionate soul, even that of a stranger, can make a difference. These victims' experiences still haunt me sometimes and I can easily get sucked into a funnel of fear. But I keep reminding myself of two things: that my volunteer work *did* make a difference and that knowing about these crimes does not make it more likely that they will happen to me.

While knowing this for myself, how do I reconcile the fear that something might happen to my child with the desire to have a normal life? For example, how do I avoid imposing draconian restrictions on my son? How can I care for the safety of my child without alienating him and unwillingly pushing him towards rebellion?

As an adventurous child and teenager with a strict mother, I was fairly rebellious and learned to trust my gut instincts. I realized again and again that when something feels not quite right, it usually is. Now, I never question any intuitive hint I get, no matter how foolish it might seem. How do I tell a gut feeling from an irrational fear? The gut feeling or intuitive hint is emotionally neutral. There is simply no emotion attached to it—no anxiety, no exaltation, just an insight. It is usually a very simple thought with no chain reaction to other thoughts. On the contrary, fear is a feeling with a physiological response, so it will never be emotionally neutral and it often causes us to spiral into other feelings and thoughts that can be even worse. As a rule, I always trust my gut but I try to question and challenge my fears.

There are several simple tricks that can help us keep our fears at bay.

We can try to stop fearful thoughts as soon as they appear by substituting them with something more empowering, by believing in miracles and by praying. We can avoid pessimistic people who like to dwell on their fears and indulge in negativity. We don't have to watch random TV programs, especially 24/7 news broadcasts; we can watch carefully chosen films, instead. We can read the news or listen to it on the radio.

We can try to make every moment of our lives as meaningful as possible and live in a way that will not cause us to have regrets later, which in many ways will require that we move beyond our fear.

We can have a list of inspirational quotes or stories in a drawer nearby and reach for them whenever we are scared or vulnerable. One of my favorite quotes is an anonymous phrase I saw somewhere that I refer to often:

"Always believe that something wonderful is about to happen."

We can help other people move beyond their fears and support them in whatever way we can. We can cheer them up, be there for them when they need to share their pain and fears, or try to uplift them. As Maya Angelou's wonderful poem "Alone" states: "Nobody, but nobody can make it out of here alone!"

So how does befriending a spider change one's perspective on life?

My mom told me a wonderful story when I was a child that I always repeat to myself whenever I am confronted with fear. A prisoner was sentenced to death by the king but decided to buy some time for himself by promising the king that if he was given one more year he would teach the king's horse to speak a human language. The king was intrigued by that offer, agreed to postpone the execution for one year and gave the man a place to sleep in his stable.

"Are you out of your mind?" asked the prisoner's friend. "How can you promise such nonsense?"

"One year is a long time and many things can happen," responded the prisoner. "For example, the king might die. The horse might die. The king might pardon me or maybe a miracle will happen and the horse will learn to speak. But in any case, I will have at least one more year to live."

So for now, Timon is learning to let go of his fear of spiders and I am enjoying a kitchen free of ants.

Diving Deeper

Everyone experiences fear at some point or another. It is part of life. But we possess a great capacity to move beyond fear—to act in spite of it, to transform what might initially stop us into motivating us to act positively and by virtue of doing so, enabling us to connect to others. These questions might help you tap your capacity for releasing some of your fears.

1. What are your little "silly" fears? How could you possibly befriend them?

2. What are some things you would love to do but are afraid of trying? Could you grow into doing some of these things by remembering Thomas Jefferson's quote: "If you want something you've never had, you must be willing to do something you've never done before."

3. Do you have any fears related to parenting that might be slightly exaggerated? Maybe you drive your child every day to an additional activity like math tutoring, chess, piano, gymnastics, etc.? Do you extensively worry about your child's future success?

Will your child be less likely to succeed if you let that fear go and lighten up a bit?

4. Can you use some of your fears as a propelling force to contribute to a tangible change in the world by helping others?

5. Do you trust your gut instincts? Can you distinguish them from fear and anxiety?

Getting Active

You may want to consider these activities to help you let go of fear in everyday situations.

1. If fear is stopping you from doing what you really want to do, like networking, public speaking, asking for a raise or pursuing a dream—try one of the following:

- Identify the thing you would really like to do. Describe the perfect outcome if you were to go for it. Read what you have written and imagine it every day. Whenever you hear the voice in your head that tells you that you should not do it, silence it by saying to your mind: "Thank you for sharing that warning but I have things to do here." Focus on your vision of the perfect outcome.

- Think of the worst case scenario and take it further by exaggerating it to the point of making it ridiculous, e.g. if I ask my boss for a raise, he or she will say "you must be kidding me," make a public announcement about my request while laughing hysterically, perform a victory dance on the table and throw some confetti on my head. How would you respond?

2. Think of something you fear that comes up once in a while and does not seem to go away for good. Close your eyes and imagine yourself standing at the ocean and holding a rock in your hands. Let yourself feel this fear and imagine it soaking into the stone. How does this fear feel? What shape, color and texture does it have? How does it smell? In which part of your body does it come up first? The more visceral and real you can make it, the better. Once the fear is quite tangible, imagine the rock as a magnet that pulls the feeling out of you. See and experience it leaving your body and saturating the rock. Once

it has entirely left your body, imagine throwing the rock into the ocean and sense the lightness and relief in your body. You can also do it with a real rock and throw it into a river, lake or ocean.

Conversation Starters to Engage Your Child

Letting Go of Fear

Sometimes I'm scared just by crossing the street,
If a big bus is coming too close to my feet.
Sometimes I'm frightened of bullies at school,
Even though bullies are not very cool.

It's normal to worry and take special care
Whenever your brain says "Look out and beware."
Say "no" to strangers; who cares if they're nice?
They may act like friends, but you better think twice.

You never can tell what a stranger might do,
If they're wearing a "mask" just to make friends with you.
If parents and teachers can't help you, just run
And, as soon as you can, you just call 9-1-1.

It's bad that the world can be so full of danger,
But kids can be smart in the path of a stranger.
I hope that no bad things will happen to you.
Be smart when you have to, and that will come true.

Getting Active Together

1. Use the poem and the illustration in the previous section to talk to your child about the necessity of being cautious with strangers. Ingrain in your child not to talk to or take anything from strangers, not to open the front door, etc. This is all leading to identify what constitutes a "healthy" sense of fear—and appropriate precautions.

2. Come up with your own version of the tale about the prisoner teaching the king's horse to talk that would be more appropriate for young children. Together you can think of additional details of the tale, more possible positive things that could come out of the given scenario. Encourage your child to draw the story.

3. Help your child befriend some of his or her fears. One way of getting started is reading Ed Emberley's book, *Go Away, Big Green Monster!* Although this book is intended for very young children, it might give you an idea for helping your child deal with some of his or her fears by deconstructing them. The book starts with an outline of a monster and by turning each page we add new elements like hair, nose, eyes, etc. and, as a result, we build the monster. Once we have done so, we un-build it by taking away the same elements with each turn of a page.

The power for creating a better future
is contained in the present moment:
You create a good future by creating a good present.

— Eckhart Tolle

13

WEAVING A SAFETY NET

I once saw a father in a restaurant having lunch with his daughter, who looked to be around eight years old. When I sat down near them, I couldn't help noticing how the father was continually preoccupied with his smart phone. His head stayed down virtually the entire time, his thumbs and fingers moving frenetically, as he appeared to be quite busy texting or searching the web, or both. I didn't know anything about their relationship or the situation at hand, but I didn't require any explanation to figure out that the adult at the table was not paying any attention to the child sitting across from him.

At first, his daughter stared at the menu as if she might be hoping it would talk back to her. Each time she raised her head, she looked at her father furtively, as if she was patiently waiting for him to finish whatever he was doing. Apparently, he never did, because for the entire time they were there—and I know this because I discreetly stalked them without a break—the father uttered just two words to his daughter.

"Daddy, can I have French fries?" the girl asked.

"Uh, yeah," he replied, barely looking up from his phone.

Somehow, when the food arrived, he managed to eat with one hand and maneuver his phone with the other, all the while not even checking in once with his daughter. For the remainder of their lunch, she just sat on her side of the booth, leaning to one side, looking through the window, seemingly stuck in the solitude of their togetherness. I had to wonder how emotionally comfortable that little girl felt that day, as she appeared to be essentially on her own.

After seeing what I think I did that day in the restaurant, it made me think twice about how I behave with my own child. While the undivided attention that father devoted to his phone may have been justified, and despite the fact that I could never imagine doing the same thing, I still had to question myself.

When interacting with Timon, am I genuinely alert or absent-minded? I try not to mentally wonder off to other lands when I'm with him, but my record of awareness and paying attention is probably mixed, at best. So while it is not my place to judge that father, it *is* good for me to hold myself accountable. Even though I don't make a habit of disappearing into my phone when I'm in a restaurant with Timon, watching that father and daughter did make me feel compelled to give Timon my undivided attention whenever we are together. Paying attention to a young child is a fundamental way to make him or her feel safe. It's the least we can do!

Since Timon was born, it seems like I have had less and less time for myself, and when I do, I'm too tired to enjoy it or use the time for something really constructive. Maybe that's because without any big chunks of uninterrupted time—at least an hour or hopefully more—it seems impossible to get any work done, be it a creative project, reading, writing, catching up on the world news, cleaning the house, going to the gym or planning a trip.

At least that's what I thought for several years after having Timon. As any parent of newborn or young children knows, it's difficult to predict how much uninterrupted time one may have on any given day—if any—so it becomes virtually impossible to plan anything or look forward to doing something with the expectation that it can actually occur.

It took me a while to realize that waiting for big chunks of time to miraculously appear was not the way to approach this dilemma. I finally came to the conclusion that I could get things done—or simply do nothing—in five, ten or fifteen minute increments. Once I saw that as a real possibility, I took every opportunity that presented itself to clean, cook, read, call, catnap, etc. I discovered that this way of living was actually not as bad as I initially predicted and surprisingly, I was able to get a lot more done than I would have expected. Juggling multiple projects in short units of time soon became my norm.

In fact, I was astounded to realize that this was actually a more enjoyable and in many ways, more productive way of working—one that fit my personality quite well. Sometimes, we become so set in our ways that we never question if we are really operating most efficiently and productively. This approach—and the attitude shift that has accompanied it—has helped me become more focused with Timon, which inevitably leads us to having more fun and feeling more satisfied with our time together.

All it takes is a dose of self-discipline and awareness. Children need quality time with their parents, some more than others, but they all want our undivided attention when we are together. That doesn't only provide an emotional safety net for them; it makes them feel important, appreciated and respected, which builds self-esteem and confidence.

If a child's needs in these areas are not met at home, this will form an empty space that they will seek to subconsciously fill by different means, such as pursuing unhealthy habits later in life or looking for the safety net among their peers. This desire to fill the inner void— while inevitable to a certain degree—can result in unhealthy habits and addictions, especially if the peer connection becomes a child's sole source of validation, attention, acceptance and adventure.

Young children like to spend time with their parents, and the older they get the more important it becomes that they associate that time with mutual trust, acceptance and fun. This begins with giving our children the feeling that they matter more than our job or other activities, that they have our undivided attention during playtime, and that we genuinely enjoy spending time with them. This does not mean that we should start trying to become their peers, abandon rules and set no boundaries. We are parents, not peers, and that should always be clear.

So how do we make more time to spend with our children? How do we give them our undivided attention when we are together? Where can we find the energy to plan for more elaborate and exciting activities? According to the Pew Research Center, today's parents find spending time with their kids more meaningful than paid work but also more energy-draining, and they find leisure activities more exciting than childcare. If we perceive being with our children as meaningful but exhausting, and because of our challenging schedules we need more leisure time to recharge, how can we spend quality time with our kids and be excited and full of energy at the same time?

I love the idea of stretching happy moments in time, a concept I discovered through Gretchen Rubin's book *The Happiness Project.* Rubin suggests that we can deepen and widen happy experiences by anticipating them more consciously, savoring every minute while we experience them, expressing our delight and cherishing the memories by recording them in any creative form we desire. Such memories can later become places of mental refuge when we need to daydream or find a cozy space in our mind.

My friend Hermann wrote once, "There is a time of waiting and a time of fulfillment." I agree. And there is beauty in the anticipation as well as in the completion and remembering of happy moments.

I have come to realize that it is important to consciously generate happy moments even though it might feel like a chore at first, especially if we would prefer to sprawl on the couch and surf the TV. This particular activity, no matter how appealing at some moments it may be, is probably not going to enrich our inventory of happy memories, nor will it add much beauty or value to our lives. We would be better off seeking something more meaningful, at least from time to time.

For example, not long ago, while enjoying a day at the pool, I wanted so badly to sit under the umbrella with my pineapple-mango smoothie and relax. The last thing I felt like doing was joining Timon and his friends in the shallow water for endless rounds of splashing and jumping. But the boys really wanted to play with a grown-up and were begging their parents to join them.

I decided to walk my talk about spending quality time with our kids and entered the water with a sigh—probably much louder than intended. I was immediately nominated to be a shark, which meant I was supposed to dive and catch the boys' feet while they were escaping. At first, the thought of scrambling under water and swallowing chlorine while trying to avoid being kicked in the head had me mentally rolling my eyes, but we ended up having a great time, myself included. Timon often refers to that day and I still smile at the memories. Was it worth giving up my perfect spot under the umbrella and not finishing my smoothie? You bet.

I heard a story recently on the radio about a man who was feeling desperate, lonely and on the verge of taking his own life.

"The only thing that kept me from jumping over the cliff," the man explained, "was the memory of my father's love, respect, understanding and support."

Weaving a secure safety net for our children is free. All it requires is time and attention.

Diving Deeper

As conscientious parents we all want to spend quality time with our children and we might sometimes struggle to do that because we are stressed, tired, or need time for ourselves. Reflecting on how we spend our time and where our hours go might help us to allocate it better.

1. How much time do you spend per week on paid work, household, childcare, and leisure? How do you divide your leisure time? Are you happy with that division?

2. Does how you spend your time reflect your values?

3. Do your children get the feeling that they matter more than your job or other free time activities or not?

4. Do you give your child undivided attention when you are together?

Getting Active

This section might help us experience and consciously create more happy moments. It might feel like a chore at first (Remember my pool experience?) but it will definitely be worth it in the long run.

1. What do you consider quality time? How does it feel? List five attributes of quality time.

2. Do you spend quality time with your children (and partner or spouse)? Describe one of the memories of having wonderful time with your family. What did you do? Who were you *being* during that time?

3. What could you do to spend more *quality* time with your child (and partner or spouse)? List five things.

4. Take time today to consciously create several happy moments by being fully present when you enjoy an activity.

5. Identify some of the "times of waiting" and "times of fulfillment" in your life. List some of the positive and enjoyable qualities of both.

Conversation Starters to Engage Your Child

Weaving a Safety Net

Sometimes the world can be kind of scary.
That's when I wish that I had my own fairy.
But with parents around, I am always secure.
If I'm hurt or feel sad, they sure have a cure.

No matter how troubled or anxious I feel,
My parents bring safety, and that is the deal.
In case I mess up or do something not clever,
I know they'll forgive me and love me forever.

Of all the emotions that anyone's known,
The scariest feeling is feeling alone.
But if you get stuck in the darkest of places,
You'll always be safe in your family's embraces.

It's such a great feeling to know you're connected
With those you can trust to be so protected.
For that, I am grateful, and confident, too.
I wish it for me and I wish it for you.

Getting Active Together

1. Plan an exciting event with your child (trip to a park, visit to a children's theatre, play date, birthday party, etc.) and keep in mind that we can deepen and widen the happy experiences by anticipating them more consciously, savoring every minute while we experience them, expressing our delight, and cherishing the memories by recording them in any creative form we desire. Try to experience all four steps with your child.

2. Encourage your child to record happy memories in various forms. This can help savor the events more deeply, remember more details, and makes for meaningful keepsakes. You can suggest to your child to collect leaves in the park to make a nature collage, shells on the beach to make wind chimes or jewelry, and rocks on a hiking trail to paint or decorate them with pompons. You can take pictures together, make a scrap book, or collect all of the relics in a nice box.

3. You can make your own version of an Advent calendar that can be used to consciously enjoy the anticipation of any fun event. You can use envelopes, small boxes, or pieces of paper with messages strung together on a yarn. You can include fun messages, clues to finding little gifts around the house, confetti, chocolate, a description of a task to be carried out, etc. You can also use this activity as a kind of scavenger hunt.

4. Encourage your child to draw, paint, write a story, or make a collage of a happy memory. Even better—do your own along with your child.

5. Try an experiment with your children. See if you can manage a cell phone free day each week.

To be fully alive, fully human, and completely awake
is to be continually thrown out of the nest.
To live fully is to be always in no-man's-land,
to experience each moment as completely new and fresh.

— Pema Chödrön

14

ACCEPTING CHANGE

"There is nothing permanent except change."

The Greek philosopher Heraclitus of Ephesus summed up the deep groundlessness of our existence in one sentence! He also captured the volatility of the realities we hold on to and the perpetual fluidity of our identity.

Maybe his maxim explains why we become distressed and confused when faced with change. We may acknowledge the change but inevitably try to run away from it by resisting, denying or distracting ourselves. Or, we may not be open to recognizing change and approach people and situations as if they permanently remain the same. In both cases, we miss the opportunities that change can bring. We either become uncomfortable and restless or we don't give ourselves—or anyone else—the chance to experience the freshness of each unique moment.

Take yesterday, for example. I had my life planned out perfectly. I was going to write this chapter on accepting change while my husband picked up Timon from school, cooked dinner, cleaned up afterwards and played several rounds of chess with our son in the evening. Bingo! Could life get any better than that? I didn't think so. But it definitely could get worse and in record time! Instead of delighting in a cup of tea while blissfully writing at my desk, I ended up spending several hours in urgent care because of an allergic reaction that left me itchy, covered with hives and gasping for air.

Luckily, it was gone after a single shot of steroids—which I waited to receive for hours and hours—but so were my plans for the afternoon and evening.

I did not write the chapter that day as planned, but my unexpected trip to the hospital perfectly illustrates the volatility of making plans and holding on to expectations. Making plans, setting goals and arranging schedules are definitely good because they provide the structure and direction we all need, but none of the projected outcomes can be set in stone. On the contrary, they may be better off written in sand. Sometimes I wonder why it is so difficult to let go of our attachment to desired results and just let life unfold with the acceptance that whatever comes will be good in one way or another.

Learning how to find comfort in volatility—not in spite of it but because of it—might be one of the steps on the path to mastering the art of joyful and inspired living.

How would it be to approach every moment and every person anew, with an openness untainted by our expectations and the ways in which we label people and situations?

As parents, we face this challenge every day with our children.

"Why do you always have to leave your shoes in the kitchen?"

"Why do you never clean up your toys?"

"Do I have to call you five times for dinner every single night?"

Does it sound familiar?

We often attach a certain image or behavior to our children that may not be entirely accurate and may simply be a result of failing to enforce limits or being lax in establishing the discipline required to affect the behavior we desire.

"Always'" and "never" and "every" are not often accurate when it comes to describing our children's habits and tendencies. We attempt to solidify things that are in flux by using these words, but more often than not they just inflame a situation instead of resolving it.

So while it is easy to label our children in certain ways, they change so fast that we are forced to adapt and acknowledge the changes. We have no choice! But when it comes to recognizing the fluidity of our own identities, it's a different story. Am I the same person I was before my son was born? Am I the same as I was two years ago or even last week?

Yes, I am and no, I am not.

On many occasions, I have desperately tried to hold on to the image I had of myself despite having already outgrown it during turning points in my life, such as coming home after spending several years abroad, an experience which usually speeds up personal transformation on many levels.

Transitions give us opportunities to embrace change, and in order to grow or accomplish anything new we have to do that. Other people may try to keep us from developing and changing because it makes them feel insecure. They want to have us remain fixed and solidified in an image that maintains their own illusions of security.

So how do we negotiate our own changes?

"Be the person you want to be."

When I first saw this on a bumper sticker, I found it profound. Why aren't more people following this advice? Many of us would like to improve or "fix" ourselves in one way or another, but that process is often postponed to an unidentified future like "next week" or "when I have more time," and the changes never seem to materialize. Why not? Why not to start creating the person we strive to be right at this moment, one choice at a time?

Will I go to that cardio class today or just sit in front of the TV?

Will I be fully present when doing a craft project with my child today, or will I keep surfing the web on my smart phone?

Will I stay stuck where I am because I have so many things I want to change and just don't know where to start?

As far as I can tell, chances are 50-50 that you'll make it to that class, connect with your kid for an hour without checking your phone or select a starting point towards change. But how would our lives life change if we kept our promises—especially the promises we make to ourselves? Don't we all teach our children to *always* keep their word?

As a "recovering perfectionist," I understand the need to be flawless and impeccable, including setting the highest standards possible and invariably beating myself up for not always living up to them. But perfectionism, as I have learned, robs us of the ability to complete or even start things we really want—and have—to do. It might be liberating to accept that imperfection, like impermanence, is part of being human.

Acknowledging the authenticity, uniqueness and value of things that are seemingly flawed and ephemeral is at the core of the Japanese concept of wabi-sabi, which I find profoundly deep and inspiring. Wabi-sabi is an acceptance and celebration of the imperfect and the incomplete; it sees beauty in a chipped bowl, a cracked sculpture, a tarnished metal piece, a broken shell, a fragmented vase and a dried leaf. It focuses on the beauty, simplicity and authenticity of the imperfect because the seemingly flawed object has a soul, a unique history and a story to tell. Wabi-sabi is also a state of mind that can help us embrace perpetual change and the cycle of life.

In spite of the resistance and unease we attach to change, it often comes exactly at the right time. Sometimes, we want things to change quickly because we feel stagnant or dissatisfied. We keep checking the mailbox, hoping for that life-changing letter. But even if we *think* that everything remains the same, it really does not because life is always changing in slow and subtle ways.

"Nothing ever goes away until it has taught us what we need to know."

This teaching from the Buddhist nun Pema Chödrön shows us how we do not let people, circumstances and situations go out of our lives until we can fully embrace what we are supposed to learn, however difficult the lessons may be. Once we can are ready, we can move on.

Years ago, I had a friend—a lovely, smart and beautiful woman—who was stuck in an abusive relationship, unable to get away from her violent and unpredictable partner. One day in utter desperation, she brought his gun to my house and asked me to keep it because she was afraid to have it around. That's when I realized how dangerous her situation had become. Obviously, she needed a drastic change, but it took Margaret more than eight years to finally end that relationship. As much as I tried to be supportive, I know that I also felt judgmental about her inability to have the guy locked up or at least kicked out of her life for good. Years later, when I discovered that most women in domestic violence situations are killed or injured *after* they separate from the perpetrator, I realized, once again, that we never really see the entire picture of another person's situation.

In other instances, change seems to happen way too fast, when we really want stability and assurance that everything will remain the same. In either case, we are very uncomfortable with uncertainty and the feeling of groundlessness.

According to Pema Chödrön, groundlessness is the lack of any certainty about the next moment and an absence of feeling connected with the nature of reality. We can believe, speculate, engage in science or even visit a psychic—but we will never know exactly what the next day will look like, nor will we know for sure how life works in its entirety. As Chödrön explains, our suffering or discomfort in life comes from our struggles to escape the feeling of groundlessness by trying to solidify and fix things that are impermanent by nature. Accepting this can help us understand our existential struggle.

Just as fear and anxiety can be contagious, so too are composure and inner peace. When Timon was about two years old, I discovered something that seemed like a great revelation to me, at least at the time. I realized that he often mirrored my emotional states. When I was stressed and agitated, he started acting out. When I was peaceful and calm, he was more cooperative. I could see and sense very clearly that he was feeding off of my behavior. Naturally, this made me want to do my best to establish and maintain a state of inner peace and remain in that place as long as possible. Some of the practices and attitudes described in the previous chapters—such as mindfulness, guided visualization, journaling or using mantras—can help create more serenity within.

Our surroundings also play an important role in supporting or hindering our ability to process change. When we surround ourselves with a tranquil and positive environment, we put ourselves in a much healthier position to embrace new challenges. Numerous studies have demonstrated that chaotic, dark and dirty places are psychologically uncomfortable and can make people more aggressive and/or depressed. Similarly, places that feel safe and psychologically comfortable are clean, organized, bright and provide some sort of pleasant stimuli. Through my own journey from depression to joyful living, I have learned that violent or sad images, dark rooms and clutter often increase gloomy moods and unhappy feelings. For years now, I have tried to set up my home in ways that support the inner states I strive to achieve—through color, light and decoration.

I learned to evoke desirable states such as tranquility, serenity or cheerfulness in living and working spaces, which helps me tune into these internal landscapes.

Examining our surroundings can help us gain additional insight into our emotional landscape, leading us to a better place for handling change. But inner peace can be compromised by unfinished projects, unkept promises—to ourselves and others—and dreams we never allow ourselves to pursue. Over time, these unfinished issues can drain our mental and emotional energy and weaken our ability to stand strong amidst the flow of life. Considering the fact that, like it or not, life does not slow down, postponement or outright abandonment of our dreams is not the best approach. If we don't create space to at least try the things we dream about, then we definitely threaten the peaceful center most of us yearn to maintain. And the only way to teach our children to do this is by doing it ourselves, one day at a time. Otherwise, it suddenly becomes too late, and then what?

It's like the advice mothers or fathers of older children often give to younger parents: "Enjoy your child now because the time goes by so quickly! You won't even realize when he or she is a grown-up."

The nostalgic flavor of this statement, combined with our own discomfort at getting older, invites a melancholic reflection about the impermanent nature of things. Change is perpetual and inevitable, yet humans continually try to hold on to a sense of stability and security, which is often an illusion or a lie we tell ourselves. This attempt to deny change—in spite of its inevitability—is one of the paradoxes of human existence.

We can do ourselves a great favor by leaving resistance at the door and focusing instead on acceptance.

Diving Deeper

Embracing change and remaining still in the midst of the storms of life is not easy, but it is definitely worth the effort. Focus on our capacity for becoming the eye of the hurricane instead of being sucked into the vortex. Let's start with these questions:

1. How would it feel for you to let go of the attachment to a desired result (at least in some situations) and just let life unfold, accepting that whatever comes will be good in one way or another?

2. How do you deal with change? Do you try to run away from it by resisting, denying, getting upset or distracting yourself? What would happen if you really embraced it?

3. Is there an image you have of yourself that might be worth letting go of in order for you to develop into a more complete version of who you are? What attitudes, circumstances or people keep you from developing and changing?

4. If the quote by Pema Chödrön, "Nothing ever goes away until it has taught us what we need to know," resonates with you on some level, can you think of any people, circumstances and situations in your life that you wish you could let go of but cannot? What could these people, circumstances and situations be trying to teach you that you are not willing to learn?

5. If you look at your home or room as a symbolic representation of your inner landscape, what does it tell you about your emotional state and your life?

Getting Active

These activities can help us develop a more flexible approach to change and encourage us to cultivate the state of inner peace and tranquility on regular basis.

Accepting Change

1. Think about last year or last month and list all the changes that took place. You might be surprised how long your list turns out to be. Choose one change that you welcomed and one that you resisted and write for 10 minutes about those experiences.

2. List some ways in which you have changed since your child was born. Write down what other changes you would like to experience.

3. Our inner peace and the ability to move forward in life can be impeded by uncompleted projects, unkept promises or dreams we never allow ourselves to pursue. List all of the unfinished issues you have in your life. Pick three from the list and make a commitment to complete them this week or month. Put the dates in your calendar, decide what the first step should be and commit to action.

4. Choose one potentially annoying person and/or uncomfortable situation. Try to approach this person or situation in a way that gives you a chance to experience the freshness and uniqueness of the moment.

5. Describe a situation in which you experienced how either fear and anxiety, or composure and inner peace, can be contagious. What can you learn from that situation?

Conversation Starters to Engage Your Child

Accepting Change

Each day my mom packs me my favorite lunch,
With food that I love and some sugar-free punch.
But one day I found something new and so strange.
What was I to do with so sudden a change?

I normally eat stuff like some pasta and sauce,
And when it's not there I sure feel a big loss.
But mom says I need to accept what comes new
And take it in stride, with no frowns or a boo.

So that's what I do because changes are fun.
That's not just for me; that's for most anyone.
At home or at school, you just never know where,
When changes make people just pull out their hair.

But changes are fun and some wishes come true.
Accept what you can and delight at the view.
Now, I'd much rather just go with the flow,
Counting my blessings and on with the show!

Getting Active Together

1. We already pay attention to yearly cycles of life by celebrating holidays, engaging in rites of passage and connecting with seasonal changes. These celebrations and customs acknowledge change but also focus on seemingly unchangeable values. They attempt to capture both the ephemeral and the eternal. Decide with your child what you are going to celebrate each month. It is easier to choose a theme or a ritual for some months than others, but stretch yourself and decide with your child how you are going to celebrate each month. Don't forget to follow up on that intent. Sketch out some ideas now.

2. Together with your child, find several objects that are seemingly imperfect. Encourage your child to experience each object in a way that allows for seeing the imperfections as a source of beauty. Imagine what story this object could tell if it could speak. Make up the story with your child. Take pictures or make a collage of these seemingly imperfect objects.

3. Embark on a project together to organize your home and/or your child's room. Add some elements that make either feel more cheerful, welcoming, happy, uplifting or serene. You could use the pictures and collages from the previous exercise.

There's nothing enlightened about shrinking so that other people won't feel insecure around you. We are all meant to shine.

— Marianne Williamson

15

BECOMING COMPLETE

Most of us yearn to make a difference in the world and want our lives to matter. We fear—often subconsciously—that our existence is of no significance, or that we have not lived up to our true potential. We all have dreams and desires that are sometimes buried and seemingly forgotten. By realizing our potential and following those dreams we can make a difference in the world. As the saying goes, what is inside you and is expressed will set you free. What is not expressed will eat you up from inside.

I had a teacher, probably in her forties, who related how she had written a letter to Nelson Mandela when she was a young girl.

"I had just learned about the struggle against apartheid in South Africa and knew that Mandela was in prison at that time," Sarah explained. "I wanted to convey how much this injustice affected me. It was a short letter written with the simplicity of a child. And I wrote that I like black people."

I smiled at our instructor.

"I got a letter back from him," Sarah continued. "He thanked me for the letter and wrote that he also likes black people."

Years later as an adult, Sarah attended one of Mandela's talks, and when she got the microphone to ask a question she also mentioned her letter.

"You must be Sarah," Mandela responded. So many years later, he still remembered Sarah's name and her genuine gesture of solidarity.

The story is beautiful and touching. At its core, we see a child's desire to make a difference in the world without questioning whether she is important enough to write to her hero. We also see a man of great stature so touched and charmed by a young girl's words.

How many grown-ups would write a letter of support to Nelson Mandela, as Sarah did? How would our lives change if we expressed the most authentic version of ourselves, as she did? If only we did not question ourselves so much and did not let other people's opinions override our own desires and intuition! If only we could drop all of the fears and limiting beliefs holding us back.

I once heard a definition of hell as a place where at the end of our lives we meet the person we could have been: the larger the gap between the actual self and our highest, unrealized potential, the greater the pain. This concept really stuck with me. Many of us do not realize our potential because it is not always easy to enter the path of self-actualization. A successful life is not measured by professional or financial success alone. Rather it is measured by integrity, the lives of other people we have touched in a positive way and our contribution to the world, be it large, medium or small.

The problem is, since we are so often conditioned to follow other people's expectations, to trust other's opinions more than our own and to conform to society's expectations, we might end up not realizing our full potential. As a matter of fact, we often need to muster up the courage to go against society's grain to find a sense of real value and completion. This path of self-realization is often scary and requires a leap of faith. Depending on our upbringing, social norms, personality and many other factors, we might be quite willing or rather hesitant to plunge into such unknown terrain. Some of us have it a little easier because our path is more conventional. Others need to chart entirely new territory as they walk an unusual trail. In either case, entering and staying on the path requires courage, determination and persistence. And because of this, we need compassion—for others and ourselves—when we get stuck or seem to be failing.

The first step is usually the most difficult, as we must tune out the noise from external influences and try to figure out what we want to do with our lives. Children have this capacity. They naturally listen to their intuition and simply follow it with enthusiasm and authenticity. It is usually we grown-ups who doubt our inner voices and teach our children to distrust or silence theirs. As children we often get emotionally hurt, close up and develop defense mechanisms such as emotional distance, or inferiority or superiority complexes, to name just a few. Then we begin to draw conclusions about the world based on our vulnerable, developing egos and a lack of deeper understanding of how life works. Many of us have ended up carrying these (usually false) beliefs around, behaving as if they are true. But we are usually not aware of these underlying beliefs until we consciously start uncovering them, and when we do—our lives change.

In my early school years, I believed that books written by women were less valuable than books written by men, probably because most of the books I had to read in my literature classes were written by males and because of the cultural conditioning of our patriarchal society that was so prevalent in mainstream culture. It did not even occur to me to challenge that belief until late in high school. I always loved writing, and who knows, maybe I would have tried to publish some of my writings much earlier had I not been shackled by this mindset. The feminist movement took up that issue long ago by pointing out that the literary canon that school children and university students were reading did not reflect the experiences, contributions and values of women and various minority groups.

Once I realized how ridiculous it all was, I started digging deeper and found a similarly irrational belief, that recognition of my achievements by women was not as important as their recognition by men. Who knows where this nonsense came from? It was probably a mixture of media messages, cultural conditioning, patriarchal society structures, family dynamics and school curriculum.

I think it is impossible to prevent children from developing all kinds of limiting beliefs, even in the most loving or supportive families as mine was. We can never fully control what conclusions our children will draw about themselves and the world as a result of interactions with family members, friends and strangers, let alone through media exposure. As parents, though, we can set a path for our children that supports faith in oneself, recognition of our feelings as valid and important, the authenticity of expression, a willingness to be vulnerable and honest, and the courage to follow one's calling.

Surely it would be much safer to embark on a personal path if we had the reassurance that we are doing the right thing. But that's not how life usually works. People who come close to realizing their full potential and who make a difference in the world devise their own plans. By figuring out our own way in life, we eventually come to realize our potential and open the door to feeling a genuine sense of completion.

This allows us to enter every situation and relationship from a place of fullness as opposed to a place that feels lacking and needy. When we feel incomplete, we are not able to create deeply fulfilling lives and relationships because we are subconsciously looking for ways to fill that inner void with other people's validation, acceptance, attention, etc. The strange thing is that when we approach other people with the (often subconscious) desire to receive from them what we feel we lack, they usually pick up on that need on an intuitive level and they either resist us, take advantage of us or run away.

Most of us probably know somebody who is desperately trying to find a date, be admired or liked—and we know how such desperate acts may end. We usually can sense whether a complement is genuine or whether it is delivered in a manipulative way. We know how it feels to receive a gift or help with strings attached; it usually has a dense, unsettling quality—very different from being asked directly and explicitly for what one needs. Don't we all usually pick up on the difference between manipulation and sincerity, between desperation and poise and between hidden agenda and honest self-expression?

Similarly, we might strive to find completion in external things and experiences that feel good. There is nothing wrong with seeking pleasure and enjoyment, of course, but coming to these experiences from a position of need may make us desperate or addicted. It is natural to want things, but approaching them in a spirit of completeness, as opposed to a spirit that is lacking, makes all the difference—often between receiving what we want or not.

We often try to get from others what we are not willing to give to ourselves: love, acceptance and recognition—things we need the most. If we loved and accepted ourselves just as we are, there would be no desperate need for others to do it instead. By the same token, we often rush to give others what we assume they need from us, because we think they cannot give it to themselves. By doing this, we soothe the wound instead of giving others space to heal them.

Becoming complete in ourselves—as opposed to waiting for other people or external circumstances to complete us—is a secret to discovering the joy within and radiating it from that internal place of fulfillment. It also requires healing any emotional wounds we may be carrying.

Completion brings fullness to every relationship and creates deep, authentic bonds. We do not have to rely on the approval of other people to feel good about ourselves, and we do not become disgruntled if we are criticized. Reaching this point takes time and work. Experiencing adverse and painful situations, despair or sorrow is part of the journey, as are happy moments, joy and excitement. When we finally understand that we do not have to be defined by outer circumstances or limited by our past experiences, we can transform our stories of victimhood and powerlessness into stories of triumph, strength and love. And when this happens, our lives become inspiring messages to the world.

The Dalai Lama once said, "If you think you are too small to make a difference, try sleeping with a mosquito." These words should help us when we question our importance or ability to make a difference. Because when all is said and done, a fulfilling life is not something that just happens; it is a choice we make every day.

Diving Deeper

We become complete by liberating ourselves from false beliefs and reclaiming the parts of ourselves that we disowned, hid or buried as a result of media messages, cultural conditioning, society structures, family dynamics, friends' influences and school curricula. The journey starts with the willingness to acknowledge that our perception of what's possible is based on a set of beliefs that are not necessarily true in their core.

1. What false beliefs do you think you might be harboring? Can you identify at least one?

2. What qualities do you express when you are at your best? How do you feel at the time of your peak performance and greatest happiness? How can you cultivate these qualities during those times when you are not functioning at that high level?

3. What is your model of the world? If it were your job to establish rules for how life works, what would they be? What is possible for you? What is not? Which of these assumptions are beliefs as opposed to reality? How can you know that they are always true?

4. How are you going to make a difference in somebody's life today?

Getting Active

These activities might help us to embark on the path to completion or at least make us somewhat aware of the places we still need to heal. If your life is not exactly as you would like it to be, there are still some places within you to heal and parts of your authentic self to re-claim.

1. Think of the values that are important to you, i.e., tolerance, respect, love, loyalty, commitment, etc. Do your relationships mirror these values? If they don't, take one step in that direction. What will that step be?

2. I read a quote encouraging me to approach every person, every experience, and even every thought with the recognition that they might shape me in ways I do not even realize or comprehend at the time. I tried it and it felt as if I was living in a different world. Can you try that for a week?

3. A wonderful life coach, Teresa Romain, suggested that I sit quietly for a while and ask myself "What do I need the most right now?" I tried this and to my surprise, it was not getting all my tasks crossed off of my to-do list. Nor was it bringing more money, more friends or more time. What came up for me was peace. And then I went through my day trying to feel more peaceful. It felt great. What do you need the most right now?

4. What are your most important values and how do you express or experience them?

   Step 1: Think for one minute what that word or concept means to you. For instance, "freedom" could feel for some people like six digits on a bank account statement while for others it would seem like skydiving. How would it feel if you had what you need the most today? What activity would accompany that feeling? Try to generate the feeling within and remember it as you go through the day.

   Step 2: Imagine a ball of light in your heart containing all of your answers. Take your time to really see it or feel it. Sense the warmth, joy and peace emanating from the ball. See the light expanding beyond your heart and body, enveloping you in a luminous glow. Throughout your day, imagine this light being right there around you.

Conversation Starters to Engage Your Child

Becoming Complete

I just heard a song that says "Be who you are."
I wonder if wishing will get me that far,
Because I'm not sure who I am or can be.
I don't have a clue how to answer my plea.

I'd like to find out all the things I can do
Beyond reading a book or just tying my shoe.
Maybe my parents can help me to know
The person inside me with room still to grow.

But there are rules—I think more than eight:
Know when to act and when to wait.
Say what you think, and do what you say.
Make your own sunshine when the sky is gray.

Choose your own views; stand up for a cause.
Have the courage to help; don't regret what was.
Do the right thing, even if it's hard.
Finish what you start and follow your heart.

Getting Active Together

1. What are some of the activities you love to engage in with your child? Which ones make you feel happy, joyful and complete? I love cuddling with my son every Saturday and Sunday morning— that's how we always start our weekend days. I love practicing piano with him and playing school, when he pretends to be my teacher. I always let him know how much I enjoy these activities and I know that he does, too. I make sure that we do them often. What do you love to do with your child? Which activities make you both feel deeply connected and joyful? Make a list and try to engage in them as much as possible.

2. Encourage your child to perform an act of kindness every week. Brainstorm and plan together what that will be.

3. Pay attention to what your child says and try to figure out if he or she has already developed any limiting beliefs. If you discover any, try to gently challenge them.

Gratitude (Acknowledgments)

This book has been shaped by many important lessons I have learned over the course of my life—some delivered with loving kindness by family, friends and strangers, and others hammered into me in emotionally painful ways. All of them shaped me to be the person I am and consequently influenced this book in many direct and indirect ways. Therefore, I am grateful for all of them: the good, the bad, and the ugly—but want to thank all of the people with joy and peace in their hearts who enriched my life in so many ways I cannot even describe. I have been very fortunate to meet so many wonderful, loving, and inspiring people that it is impossible to list them all. However, I am delighted to have the opportunity to acknowledge some for their specific contributions.

My gratitude starts with my son, Timon, without whom this book would never exist. The first idea of writing it emerged from my desire to teach him the pillars of a joyful, inspiring and fulfilling life, one similar to what I have discovered for myself and believe to contain universal principles with the power to transform individual lives and the world. I wanted to convey all of this to him in a language he could understand. From this initial idea, the project expanded into two books—one for children and the other for parents. Both books were such a joy to write and caused me to examine my own values, experiences, parenting practices, strengths and shortcomings. I realized that Timon taught me, among other things, the profound depth of unconditional love, ways to grow into a more complete and inspired mother and human being and living in the present moment without worries about past and present.

I want to thank my husband, Önder, for his love, emotional support and patience while I took time to write this book. I am grateful for his wisdom, compassion towards other people, high ethical standards and his inquisitive, analytical mind. He taught me to look at life from multiple perspectives at once.

Two people shaped the content and structure of this book in such profound ways that it would not be the same wonderful book without their wisdom, support, dedication and skills: my dearest friend and soul sister, Jeanne Batalova, and one of the best editors on earth, David Tabatsky.

Jeanne has been a wonderful friend during the past fifteen years. She has never failed me and always provided unwavering support in all matters—big and small. I am grateful for our weekly writing sessions, exchange of ideas, feedback on each chapter, encouragement at every step of this project, guidance through the logistics of publishing and marketing, blog help and technical support in all matters related to social media. A trailblazer in many ways, Jeanne is not only a member of my family, but also a big part of this book.

David's editing genius propelled this book forward in many wonderful ways I did not expect or imagine before. The book really took off after we started working together and I attribute being able to write it almost entirely during three summer months to our cooperation. David shaped my original poems into their current version with poetic spirit, lightness and humor. I am grateful for his amazing editing mind and skills and his dedication to this book. He is such a big part of this book and I cannot imagine it coming to life without him.

I want to thank my friends who took time to read parts of the book and offer feedback. Uluç Bayar—for his enthusiasm and such genuine desire to help me improve my book; Ivett Guntersdorfer—for her caring about this project so much and really understanding its essence; Chuck Hammond—for very detailed and honest feedback.

I have always admired his sense of social justice and the courage to express his progressive political views; Simona Moti—for being able to relate to this book in a very personal way; Ania Uryga—for bringing me back to reality from the utopia of parenting and for the picture (many pictures); Diana Wendel—for sharing her parenting experience and wisdom; and Kirsten Zoub—for encouraging me to follow my heart.

My mom, Ewa, has been impatiently waiting for this book, always encouraging me and believing in me. She also provided valuable feedback and helped me make smart decisions that eventually led to the successful completion of this project. Thank you for always providing unwavering support, raising me with so much love, being proud of me, and giving me hope when I needed it the most.

I also want to acknowledge my family and friends who contributed to this book in indirect but important ways—by playing a big role in my life.

My stepfather, Rysiu, has been always very supportive and became Timon's best friend and partner-in-play. His unparalleled sense of humor brought us unforgettable moments of laughter. The goodness of his heart has been a source of joy and inspiration.

My brother, Romek, could always make me laugh, even when I thought I could not even smile. Being able to be silly and completely myself around him has taught me the delight of lightheartedness and has given me a lot of confidence. Our mutual trust and caring are invaluable in my life.

I want to thank my father, Andrzej, for his deep love and for teaching me not to be afraid. He set high standards for me and always wanted me to succeed. I am grateful for his caring and always doing his best. I would have not been where I am in my life without his support.

My step-mother, Hella, has been a role model for me in terms of optimism and her cheerful approach to life. She taught me to be buoyant and always look for the bright side of things. A source of encouragement for many years, Hella provided uplifting wisdom and kind support.

I want to remember my grandparents, without whom I would not be who I am today. My grandmother Roma—who loved me so much; my grandfather Marian—who instilled in me the love of adventure; my grandfather Władzio—who introduced me to the world of art; and my grandmother Bunia—who cared so deeply about me.

I also want to remember Patti Leviton, a dear mentor, who showed me many new ways of thinking, being, and relating to the world. She will always be in my heart.

I am indebted to Cheryl Cozad, Grażyna Mancewicz, and Celine Jacquemin, some of the helping hands mentioned in Chapter 6.

I want to thank the team at the Author House for helping me with all the logistics of manuscript submission, editing, and publishing. I am especially grateful to John Carter, Jean Bray, and Timothy Murphy. Big thanks to Rachel Fogg of Comma Down for the last minute proofreading.

Finally, my colleagues, teaching assistants, students and staff at UCLA enabled me to experience the unsurpassed joy of teaching, academic and personal growth and inspiration—all of which influenced this book in many ways.

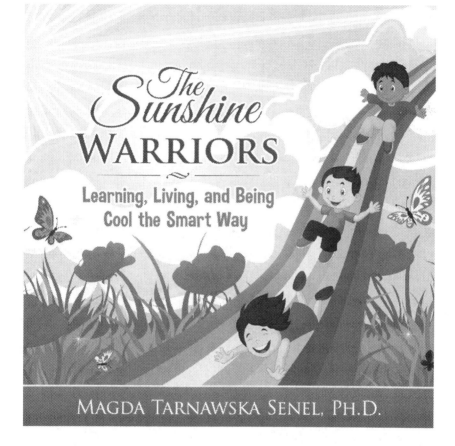

This delightful companion book to *Be the Wisdom You Want to See in Your Kids* is a children's version of this book, featuring the poems included here and the same illustrations, but in living color. It can be purchased separately at http://thinkjoyactpeace.com/, on Amazon, or in any bookstore.

WELCOME TO MY WEBSITE AND BLOG!

http://thinkjoyactpeace.com/

If you found this book appealing, please visit my website and blog, dedicated to inspiring and empowering people to create more joy and peace within themselves and in the world.

Printed in the United States
By Bookmasters